AF245610

REVOLUTIONS
a Collaboration

JOHN MATTHIAS

JEAN DIBBLE

ROBERT ARCHAMBEAU

DOS MADRES

2017

DOS MADRES PRESS INC.
P.O.Box 294, Loveland, Ohio 45140
www.dosmadres.com   editor@dosmadres.com

Dos Madres is dedicated to the belief that the small press is essential to the vitality of contemporary literature as a carrier of the new voice, as well as the older, sometimes forgotten voices of the past. And in an ever more virtual world, to the creation of fine books pleasing to the eye and hand.

Dos Madres is named in honor of Vera Murphy and Libbie Hughes, the "Dos Madres" whose contributions have made this press possible.

Dos Madres Press, Inc. is an Ohio Not For Profit Corporation and a 501 (c) (3) qualified public charity. Contributions are tax deductible.

Executive Editor: Robert J. Murphy

Illustration & Book Design: Elizabeth H. Murphy
www.illusionstudios.net

Typset in Adobe Garamond Pro & Cambria
ISBN 978-1-939929-74-7
Library of Congress Control Number: 2017935338

Paid permission for use of Osip Mandelstam photos from
Alamy Stock Photos.

First Edition

Revolutions: A Collaboration.
Table of Contents.

Epilogue: The Hij's Happy Book of Insults

After Five Words Englished from the Russian

John Matthias

1. Haphazard

       is the method of the new hussars;
the tsar's unhappy; bless him

and applause aplenty bring to his tsarina.
All bells toll this inauspicious hour.

Peasant absentee shuns orthodoxy of
the Bishop of Pah. It reigns down from clouds

O hallelujah crowd and ever after: Winds blow
across the steppe, the messenger

caught up in mass and mission
fails in the individual soul: Everything's for sale,

especially oil, soil. Ahph! Our brother's pipeline
sabotaged by cabbage claims. Borsht!

Poetics is no longer worth a pension
even for a splaygirl in from Budapest. Anapests –

the three red accents on her breasts.
Hazard me a guess, dauntless guest of hap-

penstance drinking vodka at our happy hour.
That was the moment. That was the power.

Hapax Legoman was his love, who
drove a nine and twenty for her dower.

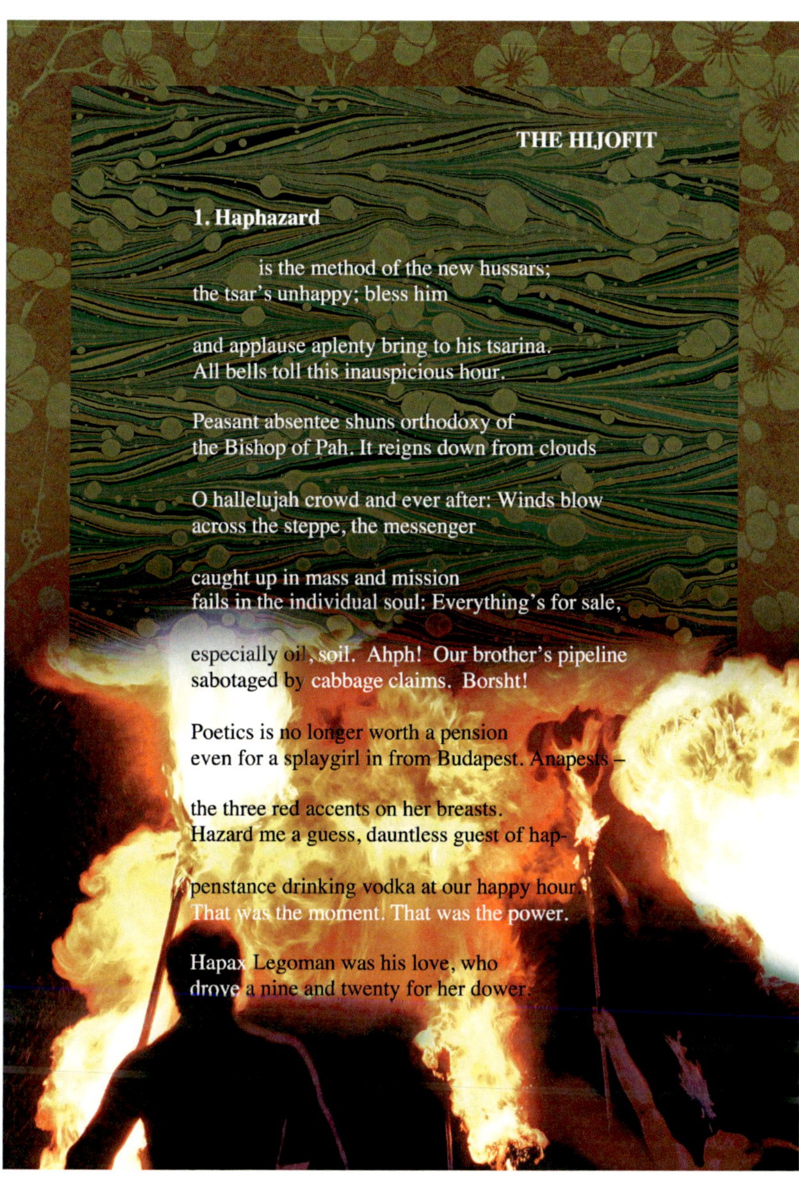

1. Haphazard

is the method of the new hussars;
the tsar's unhappy; bless him

and applause aplenty bring to his tsarina.
All bells toll this inauspicious hour.

Peasant absentee shuns orthodoxy of
the Bishop of Pah. It reigns down from clouds

O hallelujah crowd and ever after: Winds blow
across the steppe, the messenger

caught up in mass and mission
fails in the individual soul: Everything's for sale,

especially oil, soil. Ahph! Our brother's pipeline
sabotaged by cabbage claims. Borsht!

Poetics is no longer worth a pension
even for a splaygirl in from Budapest. Anapests –

the three red accents on her breasts.
Hazard me a guess, dauntless guest of hap-

penstance drinking vodka at our happy hour.
That was the moment. That was the power.

Hapax Legoman was his love, who
drove a nine and twenty for her dower.

H is for Haslam's *History*

Who are they, then, these new hussars? And who's the windblown messenger caught up in mass and mission? Who, also, is our brother, and who the splaygirl come from Budapest? "Hazard me a guess," we hear. I'll hazard this: they're all from Haslam's *History*, or close enough. Dull critic that I am, I won't mimic Matthias, no. No, I'll explain.

Silas Haslam's *History of the Land Called Uqbar* exists only in one place—or three, depending how you count the reality of immaterial things. For the most puritanical of enumerators, it exists only in a story by Jorge Luis Borges, "Tlön, Uqbar, Orbis Tertius." The hero of that story comes across a mention of Haslam's *History* in the bibliography appended to the last article of a stray volume of the fictitious 1917 *Anglo-American Encyclopedia*, an imaginary illegal reprint of the eminently real *Encyclopedia Brittanica* of 1903. This imagined version of a real book is, in fact, the second place, other than Borges' story itself, where Haslam's book stakes its tenuous claim to reality. But the encyclopedia article that mentions Haslam faces great challenges in its claim to existence: besides being a construct of Borges' imagination, it is apocryphal even within the story born of that imagination. There, it exists only in the possibly unreliable testimony of a secondary character— some copies of the encyclopedia lack the article, and we have only the testimony of this character to indicate that at least one copy does indeed contain four extra pages describing Uqbar.

Strangely, Haslam's *History* has a greater claim to existence than the encyclopedia article in which it is mentioned, as characters in the story discover it mentioned in the catalog (the third place of its existence) of a bookshop. To be precise, they discover it in the catalog of Bernard Quartich's bookshop— a real shop, opened in London in 1847 and open there still.

Whether Haslam's book ever existed in the catalog of the venerable Quartich's, I cannot say. Doubts abound, but scholars have yet to assemble the catalogs of Quartich, dispersed as they have been over the globe for a hundred and sixty years and more. So we just don't know for sure.

But H is not just for Haslam's *History*, nor for "Haphazard," "nor 'Hig' nor 'Hijofit'." H is also for "Hermeneutic code." Of the five communicative codes described in Roland Barthes' *S/Z*, this is the one that most frustrates and satisfies readers. It refers to those elements of narrative that are not explained, that raise enigmas and set us hunting for answers. Sometimes, as in the detective story, we find those answers, our hermeneutic hunger satisfied with a great "aha!" But sometimes an author—wily, sly, or incompetent—frustrates us in our search. Sometimes they make us fall into what Barthes calls a "snare"—an enigma refusing to be resolved.

We might say that the reality of Haslam's *History* in Borges' story is a snare. Except that Borges is more wily still. His story isn't just about the dubious existence of things—it is about the influence of nonexistent things, their propensity to multiply and become real. Through machinations too arcane to articulate here, artifacts not of Uqbar, but of Tlön—a fictitious realm from the literature of Uqbar—begin to manifest as actual objects in the real world of Borges' story. What was caught in the hermeneutic snare is unleashed in the world itself. If you don't believe it, try Googling "Uqbar" or "Haslam's History." You'll find they're mentioned, now, not in one place, or three, but many thousands. Borges sent them from the narrow valley of the unsubstantial to the broad fields of ubiquity.

Who, then, are Matthias' hussars? And who's the windblown messenger? We don't know who they are. But we know where they are: they're in three places. They're caught in the

poet's snare—from which none of them shall escape to make a
horseman's charge, or deliver a messenger's missive. And they're
in an artist's image, in colors they never knew or wore. And
they're in this commentary, now. They are snared and stuck
forever, and they begin to travel.

2. *Indenture*

       is indefinite to articles;
Madame is indecent; *any* we might say enough?

Or *some* things. Her dayglow spikeheel shoes
are on, although her clothes are off.

On-off. As though one clicked a light switch
several times. Or in-out. He wrote for

the dispatch but wasn't articled in *n.2:* a contract
or a deed; *tr.v:* to bind in function of

derivative: $\int f(x)dx + C$ where C's the arbitrary
constant. She did indeed love *me* though *he*

sought indemnity for integrals
where $\int f(x)dx$ was any member of her set.

The poems they wrote to her about her
index of refraction! No one knew she was

indebted to the tsar. She was indicative.
Indelibles suggest an assignation with the prince,

the princess, and the handsome slave.
In the end she was

      indented   & indicted everywhere
courting nine and twenty to her grave.

2. Indenture

is indefinite to articles;
Madame is indecent; *any* we might say enough?

Or *some* things. Her dayglow spikeheel shoes
are on, although her clothes are off.

On-off. As though one clicked a light switch
several times. Or in-out. He wrote for

the dispatch but wasn't articled in *n.2:* a contract
or a deed; *tr.v:* to bind in function of

derivative: $\int\!f(x)dx + C$ where *C*'s the arbitrary
constant. She did indeed love *me* though *he*

sought indemnity for integrals
where $\int\!f(x)dx$ was any member of her set.

The poems they wrote to her about her
index of refraction! No one knew she was

indebted to the tsar. She was indicative.
Indelables suggest an assignation with the prince,

the princess, and the handsome slave.
In the end she was

indented   & indicted everywhere
courting nine and twenty to her grave.

I is for in the beginning

"In the beginning," John Matthias once wrote, "without any mother the girl was born a machine."

Those words began the long poem "Working Progress, Working Title," and one might be forgiven if one is bewildered by the content even as one is bewitched by the rhythm. The referent is, in fact, a bit fuzzy beneath those compelling dactyls. In one sense, it could be said to be the presiding spirit of the more machine-oriented, futuristic types of modern art—the high art of Antheil's *Ballet Mécanique* and the popular art of early film alike: one imagines this girl as the *Maschinenmensch*, the robot-woman in Fritz Lang's *Metropolis*. In another sense, the girl born a machine can also be someone more particular—Claire Lescot, the heartless lead character in Marcel L'Herbier's 1924 film *L'Inhumaine*. That film included contributions by what amounts to a long roll call of the leading names in Modernist painting, dance, design, music, and architecture—and Matthias, in his "Working Progress," soon makes a similar roll call of Modernism: "Voilà Picabia sweetheart of first/occupation voilà ballet mécanique," he writes; or, later, "Antheil Olga Boski Hedy and Ez, she says:/ Or probably better/Olga and Ez, Antheil and Boski." It's as if Matthias is on intimate terms with Antheil and Pound and Picabia and their wives, a member of their circle. So who is Matthias in relation to that girl who was born a machine? Just any member of her set.

The members of the set in "Indenture" are, of course, members of an integral set, part of the calculus whose equations Matthias writes for their music. The integrals are part of the dictionary game Matthias has set for himself in "The Hijofit," a game whose pieces are the first few nine-letter words he finds in a dictionary's listing under a given letter. But I'm only interested in getting to the import of these integrals by

a back way—by reference to the set Matthias really loves: the
Modernists. His poetry, an unsympathetic critic once said, was
"just Modernism." Wrong in her dismissiveness (can dismis-
siveness ever be right?) she was right to sense the Modernism in
Matthias. Not only is his work written in accord with a thou-
sand Modernist techniques—the jump-cut, the arcane allusion,
the geo-cultural rock-drill, to name just a few—it constantly
invokes the Modernists themselves: the poets, the artists, and
especially the composers. He knows their lives, their works, the
failings, follies, and glories, and obsesses over them. I mean,
I've heard him talk. But about this obsession one asks: why?

Because I is also for "isolation." There had been alien-
ated artists before the twentieth century, but nothing like what
we find among the Modernists. Exiled or expat, bohemian
in habit, radically advanced and challenging in form and
views, they are our icons of the unpopular arts. "Production
for producers," say the Marxists, noting how painters sold to
other painters, and poets wrote for few but their poetic peers.
L'Herbier hoped his film would showcase modern art for the
masses—but it was greeted with jeers as great as those he'd
filmed for the scene where a crowd turns against the cold-
hearted Claire Lescot. It was a moment worthy of Borges—a
fictional moment that made itself happen for real. Matthias is
drawn to the lives and works of the Modernists because they
speak to the condition of all non-, or anti-commercial artists
who have come after them. They are the patron saints, the
forefathers, the ones who got here first. By "here" I mean that
special island where we refuse to compromise, to bend our art
to serve the powers (we who won't be indebted to the Tsar) or
fit the common taste. And when we step aside from trying to
win patrons or sell tickets, we find that those we're left with are
those who love the art as art, and especially those who love the
medium itself—materials and form.

Which is why I is also for "impasto," the thickness of the built-up paint. "The use of impasto," I read once in a catalog from the Tate,

> …became more or less compulsory in modern art as the view took hold that the surface of a painting should have its own reality rather than just being a smooth window into an illusionist world beyond. With this went the idea that the texture of paint and the shape of the brushmark could themselves help to convey feeling, that they are a kind of handwriting that can directly express the artist's emotions or response to the subject.

And in "Indenture" is impasto—of words, if not of paint. The dictionary games, the echoes of the vowel "i," the fading of the referent to make room for the sounds of words: this is Matthias' impasto. His integral sets are here because a love of language just as language guides the words he types. He'll discover things within the matrix of his mechanical game of selected words. And the discoveries will be a kind of handwriting expressive of his emotions or his response to his subject. A modernist response: mechanical, expressive. A modernist response bewildering to most.

In the beginning without any referent, the poem was born a machine.

3. Jerkwater

   town's the home of Jeroboam
who is aquarius to every passing phantom train.

Houses are jerrybuilt and shake like Jericho
when jayhawker nightfreights come arumbling through.

The Jews, the Gentiles there. The arbitrary constant C
was married to an Imam, tsar and all

his retinue forgotten. It was far away.
Jesuits are exiled to Australia – to Jarvis Bay,

you Jerk! said Mr. Waters. Indenture and Haphazard
were his favorite words. Herds of Yahwists

streaming toward Jerusalem and jet set derivatives
of $\int f(x)dx$ expired in a desert without wells.

I'm well enough, said Jeroboam, *thank you very much.*
Ahph! Borsht! They should have come by train

where hallelujah crowd and everafter jerk
their waters to attain the wherewithal for steam.

Spare us any jeremiad. Everything's explained
by a damned outrageous jealousy:

Hapax Legoman more a Jezebel than Judith,
nine and twenty for a faithless C.

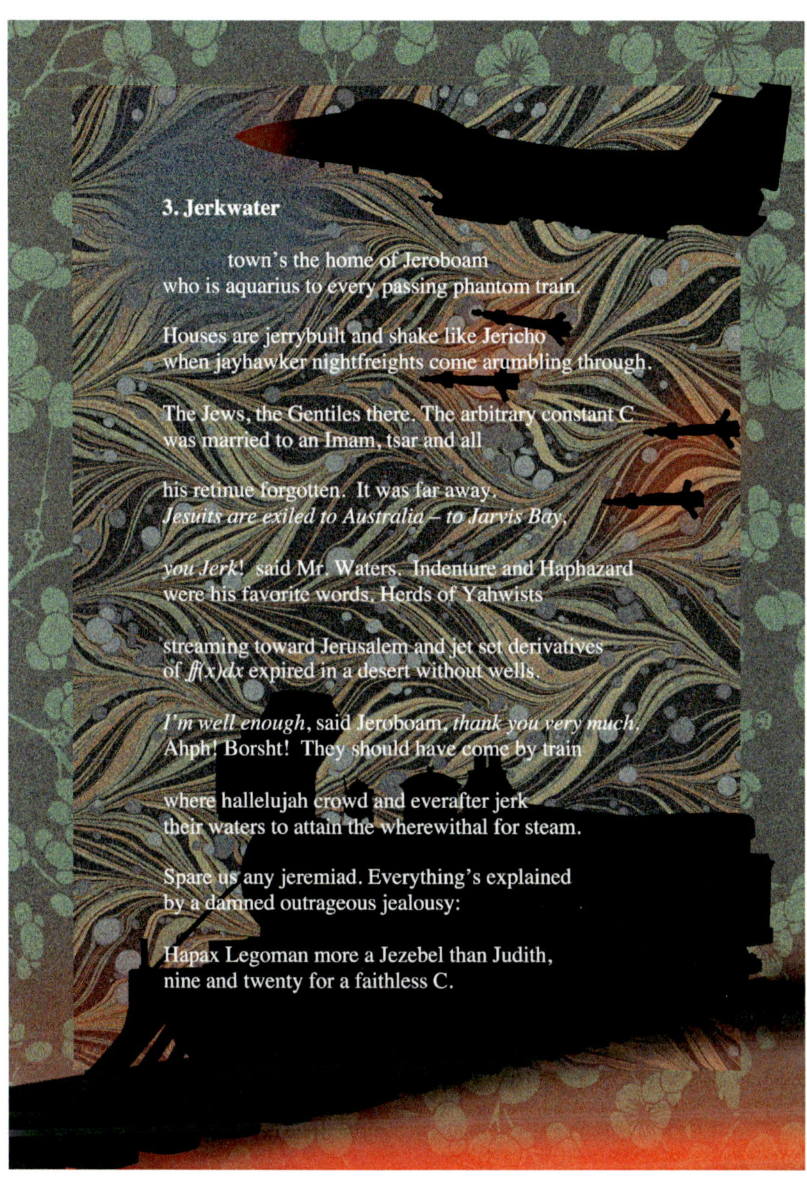

3. Jerkwater

          town's the home of Jeroboam
who is aquarius to every passing phantom train.

Houses are jerrybuilt and shake like Jericho
when jayhawker nightfreights come arumbling through.

The Jews, the Gentiles there. The arbitrary constant C
was married to an Imam, tsar and all

his retinue forgotten. It was far away.
Jesuits are exiled to Australia – to Jarvis Bay,

you Jerk! said Mr. Waters. Indenture and Haphazard
were his favorite words. Herds of Yahwists

streaming toward Jerusalem and jet set derivatives
of $\int\!\!\int f(x)dx$ expired in a desert without wells.

I'm well enough, said Jeroboam, *thank you very much.*
Ahph! Borsht! They should have come by train

where hallelujah crowd and everafter jerk
their waters to attain the wherewithal for steam.

Spare us any jeremiad. Everything's explained
by a damned outrageous jealousy:

Hapax Legoman more a Jezebel than Judith,
nine and twenty for a faithless C.

J is for Jakobson

<blockquote>

Linguist Linda R. Waugh has a lot of questions:

What is it that differentiates a poetic text from a non-poetic text? What makes poetic discourse different in kind from other types of discourse? In other words, what are the *intrinsic linguistic properties* of the text which makes it a poem: what is there about the *internal structure* of a poem which announces it as a poem?

</blockquote>

And Roman Jakobson has one big answer, equipped with an equally large qualification:

<blockquote>

The set toward the message as such, focus on the message for its own sake, is the poetic function of language…. Any attempt to reduce the sphere of poetic function to poetry or to confine poetry to the poetic function would be a delusive oversimplification. Poetic function is not the sole function of verbal art but only its dominant, determining function, where as in all other verbal activities it acts as a subsidiary, accessory contingent. This function, by promoting the palpability of signs, deepens the fundamental dichotomy of signs and objects.

</blockquote>

So, then: a poetic function, defined as an emphasis on the verbal message in itself, may be found anywhere. It dominates poetry, but does not exhaust it.

So, then: "jerkwater," and "jayhawker," so "Jerusalem." The nine letter words beginning with J Matthias dug up from his dictionary.

So, for good measure "Jericho," "jerrybuilt," "Jews,"
"Jesuits," and" "Jarvis Bay," "jeremiad," "jet set," "Jezebel" and
"Judith." It's not like you'll miss the pattern of alliteration, even
if you're not paying attention.

So "Jerkwater," the third section of Matthias "The
Hijofit," is, like "Haphazard" and "Indenture," governed by
an arbitrary restriction or obstruction chosen with the spe-
cific goal of foregrounding the verbal surface of the text. The
restriction forces the poet to accommodate his narrative to the
words dredged up in his net, and forces the reader to notice the
restriction, and the poet's dexterity in working around it.

Poetry has been defined many ways: for Philip Sidney
it was a neo-Platonic golden world, found only in the zodiac of
the poet's wit; for William Wordsworth it was the language of
a man speaking to men—a non-specialist in a time of creep-
ing specialization. But Jakobson's definition of what counts as
poetic is a modern one, a definition fit for a time when all the
arts put their media forward as their essence.

Surely the foregrounding of language, of the message
itself, its sound-echoes and alliterations, doesn't exhaust the
entirety of "The Hijofit." But one thing "The Hijofit" makes
entirely clear is that Matthias is a modern poet.

The message for its own sake first. The Tsar and all his
retinue? Almost forgotten.

1. Deficient

> and degenerate, the Hij was defrauded
by Defiance. HIJ: he liked to go by his initials like

the FDRs and JFKs, although he was Republican.
Republic was deformed when the Hij was out

beyond the limit of his sums: broken definite integral
left him no degrees. It pained him and

he called on: Defoe, De Gaulle, Degas, et. al. But they
weren't any help at all. Afph! Borsht!

They'd degrade his forces with artillery and fix
bayonets to break his squares, but he was pretty cool:

All roots were cubed in his ice tray. *Just water, Hij,*
said A.J. Haphazard. *I'll defray your costs if*

You return the article you took from my degree.
Thee and Thou were both defrocked

before arriving here and now so wholly *dégagé.*
They'd defer the whole damned thing

provided biwings weren't already in the air
defoliating forests, model nine and twenty firing

tracers over Jerkwater's vast degaussing works.
The last definition: "Busted Billionaire."

THE DEFITCIT

1. Deficient

          and degenerate, the Hij was defrauded
by Defiance. HIJ: he liked to go by his initials like

the FDRs and JFKs, although he was Republican.
Republic was deformed when the Hij was out

beyond the limit of his sums: broken definite integral
left him no degrees. It pained him and

he called on: Defoe, De Gaulle, Degas, et. al. But they
weren't any help at all. Afph! Borsht!

They'd degrade his forces with artillery and fix
bayonets to break his squares, but he was pretty cool:

All roots were cubed in his ice tray. *Just water, Hij,*
said A.J. Haphazard. *I'll defray your costs if*

You return the article you took from my degree.
Thee and Thou were both defrocked

before arriving here and now so wholly *dégagé*.
They'd defer the whole damned thing

provided biwings weren't already in the air
defoliating forests, model nine and twenty firing

tracers over Jerkwater's vast degaussing works.
The last definition: "Busted Billionaire."

D is for Donald

The critic Brian McHale once wrote of a lamentable tendency among those who comment John Ashbery's digressive long poem "The Skaters":

> Unlike the more obviously disjunctive poems of Ashbery's *Tennis Court Oath* period, "The Skaters" often appears to make sense locally, inviting the reader to expect to make global sense of the poem. Instead, one encounters an intractable flux of verbal "found objects," shifting styles and registers, teasing literary allusions and echoes, fragmentary narrative episodes and descriptive scenes. How is one to negotiate or manage such flux? Critics tend to select "key" lines or passages, treating these as interpretative centers or "nodes" around which to organize the heterogeneous materials of the poem. Other materials come to be subordinated in various ways (explicitly or, more often, implicitly) to these "key" passages or are simply passed over in silence, so that the poem is reduced to a skeletal structure of points that yield most readily to a particular interpretative orientation.

For McHale, the suppression of disparate elements in order to create a simplified and false representation of Ashbery's poem was a critical failure, one repeated in different forms on many occasions.

*

"Go," the Danish filmmaker Lars von Trier commanded, "to the most miserable place in the world." He was speaking on camera, to another filmmaker, Jorgen Leth, who had accepted von Trier's challenge to re-shoot his film *The Perfect Human* under a variety of conditions. The resulting film, *The Five Ob-structions,* showcases Leth's ingenuity in meeting with a variety of strictures: to remake his film as a cartoon, to remake it with no set and no shot lasting more than twelve frames, and so on. But the most difficult challenge wasn't technical, but ethical: to reshoot the film in a place of deep misery, but to give no sense whatsoever that it had been shot there, to conceal the misery surrounding the film crew on all sides. Leth proceeded to the red light district of Mumbai, but could not bring himself to follow von Trier's instructions: he reshot the film with the immiserated people of the district visible in the background. Lars von Trier considered this a failure.

*

I will now fail.

*

I write this in late November of 2016, in America. That is: I write in a country that, barring miraculous deliverance, is about to be led by the most demagogic, most arbitrary, most authoritarian and least fit man ever to take on the role of President. To write without acknowlegment of that fact is something I cannot do, so I will fail to follow the constraints of critical writing (already somewhat in abeyance). I will fail in the sense that Leth failed von Trier. I will also fail in the sense that Ashbery's critics have failed McHale: I will comment on Matthias' poem by selecting exactly those "key" passages or "nodes" that allow me to distort and simplify the poem in support of a reading that an appreciation of the poem as a whole would not support.

So my thesis is this: Matthias' poem is about Donald Trump.

21

Consider: the lingering presence of authoritatian Russians.

Consider: the splaygirl from Europe (east), her spike heels on, her clothing off.

Consider: the shunning of orthodoxy, the haphazardness, the applause.

Consider: everything's for sale, especially oil.

Consider (looking forward): indictment everywhere.

Consider: jet-set derivatives.

Consider (he's not Manhattan—he comes from Queens): everything's explained by a damned outrageous jealousy.

Consider: deficient and degenerate.

Consider: (not Defoe, and not Degas)—DeGaulle.

Consider: defoliating forests (soon).

Consider, consider and condemn, at last: D is for Donald, our Busted Billionaire.

2. Eidolonie

        was elected by an acclamation
as "the most likely to succeed," although she

neither spelled properly nor could pronounce
the name of their assembly: *Eisteddfod.*

Illya Grigorievich, Dwight David, Karl Adolf: all
filled in the Es, as did Alexander Gustave.

Eiger Alp is taller than the Eiffel Tower by some
12,000 feet. Eidolonie said: *you may ejaculate, my dear,*

but don't come to my place. Her lover was eidetic,
E.D. Eidetic, his E.T.C. irregular

as waves rolled in at two or three megahertz
above the atmosphere on Elba,

the E layer breaking up a classified transmission
all through the Tuscan Archipelago.

The Hij was no Napoleon although he always
kept his right hand in his shirt, sent

his mail ewards, took care to use the secret moniker
as *nom de guerre,* drawing out

his nine and twenty to defend the honor of a lady
he knew nothing yet about.

2. Eidolonie

    was elected by an acclamation
as "the most likely to succeed," although she

neither spelled properly nor could pronounce
the name of their assembly: *Eisteddfod*.

Illya Grigorievich, Dwight David, Karl Adolf: all
filled in the Es, as did Alexander Gustave.

Eiger Alp is taller than the Eiffel Tower by some
12,000 feet. Eidolonie said: *you may ejaculate, my dear,*

but don't come to my place. Her lover was eidetic,
E.D. Eidetic, his E.T.C. irregular

as waves rolled in at two or three megahertz
above the atmosphere on Elba,

the E layer breaking up a classified transmission
all through the Tuscan Arcapelago.

The Hij was no Napoleon although he always
kept his right hand in his shirt, sent

his mail ewards, took care to use the secret moniker
as *nom de guerre*, drawing out

his nine and twenty to defend the honor of a lady
he knew nothing yet about.

E is for editorial

The editor may condense, organize, correct, amend, and collaborate. The editor's methods may be more or less precise. The editor can, among other things, annotate. As, for example:

Eidolon: From the Greek *eidos,* meaning "form or "idea." An ideal being, one that is idealized. Sometimes a spirit or a projection from an absent being, such as Helen, whom, as Homer implies and Euripedes affirms, was never physically present in Troy at all. An Eidelone is *hapax legomenon,* a term found only in a single text, in this case: this text. Who is Eidelone? She is an Eidolon, projected, female, and ideal. She is here and nowhere else.

Eisteddfod: From the Welsh, with roots in the words *eistedd,* meaning "sit," and *bod,* meaning "be," the term referred to the Bardic gatherings sponsored by Rhys ap Gruffydd, warlord of Deheubarth in southern Wales in the twelfth century. In the eighteenth century the term was revived to designate musical and literary festivals, and the usage continues to this day. Only a purely speculative etymology links the "sit-be" with the notion of visiting musicians "sitting in" on a jam session. Only a more fantastic speculation could create an Eisteddfod of electors who choose Eidolonie as most likely to succeed.

Ehrenburg, Ilya Gigorievich: Soviet author of more than a hundred books, the most renowned of them, *The Thaw,* so influential as to name an era in post-Stalin Soviet history; the best of them, *Black Book,* deadly honest in chronicling the Soviet genocide of Russia's Jews. An author virtually unknown to the broad Western reading public today.

Eisenhower, Dwight David: A man of immense power and modest gifts as a painter. His portrait—commissioned by Major General John Scully, a man of immense power, and executed by a painter of modest gifts—looms over the main stairway of the Union League Club in Chicago, a stairway I climb when meeting John Matthias for lunch in the oak paneled confines of his club. By which I mean: his wife, Diana's, club. One must sign a pledge of loyalty to the nation to become a member, and Matthias will not sign.

Eichmann, Karl Adolph: *Obersturmbannführer* of the S.S., and a byword for those who sign on and do as they are bid by duty, however black the evil, however dark the deed. There are a thousand Eichmanns of a thousand names in Ehrenburg's *Black Book*, and more than a few who followed Eisenhower, Rhys ap Gruffydd too.

Eifell, Alexander Gustave: The man who built a bridge sideways in the air in France. One may climb 1,710 steps to the top and not encounter a single portrait of Eisenhower, but the power of the army is felt nevertheless. French authorities were to raze the tower for scrap until Eifell proposed erecting an antenna at the top to send and receive radio messages for the military. Today more than a hundred antennae cover the tower, broadcasting messages undreamed of by any *Maréchal de France.*

Eiger Alp: This mountain is accessible only to the most experienced of climbers, although the creators of the Jungfrau railroad have, through their efforts in engineering a line with viewing stations, made it possible to see the best sights on offer without having to make the climber's effort. They are the editorial annotators of the Eiger Alp.

Eidetic: Should one choose to read this as a noun (I do), it refers to one who may form mental images and see them hovering before him, as if actually there. An Eidetic viewing an eidolon of a lascivious nature might indeed ejaculate, but the Eidolon not being truly present (see Homer and Euripedes on Helen of Troy) could not, through any effort of exertion, come on her face. It is surely of this that the poet wrote.

E layer: An atmospheric level in which radio transmissions make their way beyond the horizon.

And of "Eidolonie," then? This entire Eisteddfod is an eidolon, and Matthias the irregular eidetic. His E layer transmitting a more than modest art afar, out above a world of Ehrenburgs and (let's not forget) a world of Eichmanns too.

3. Facsimile

        was no part of that faction, although
he went to meetings once.

Eidolonie said he was forgotten, but that was just
a ruse to get him off the factory floor.

What a factor he become; complete fabrication of the Hij
and sourced in many fabliaux, he was a facer

when it came to ascertaining his intent. He was more
factitious than facetious in the end, and that

enabled penetration of their code. Oh, his secret was
his love for Eidolonie, his posture on

the postage stamp a provocation had it not said
E.D. Eidetic underneath the photograph.

His face, alas, looked quite aristocratic, so they
broke his nose and cut off all his hair.

He was an heir to the ages. That's why they hated him.
They hatted him with bowler first and then

with *bonnet rouge.* His original eventually was lost
among the more than ninety facets

of the compound insect eye with which they stared
at him: bent and starved and only twenty nine.

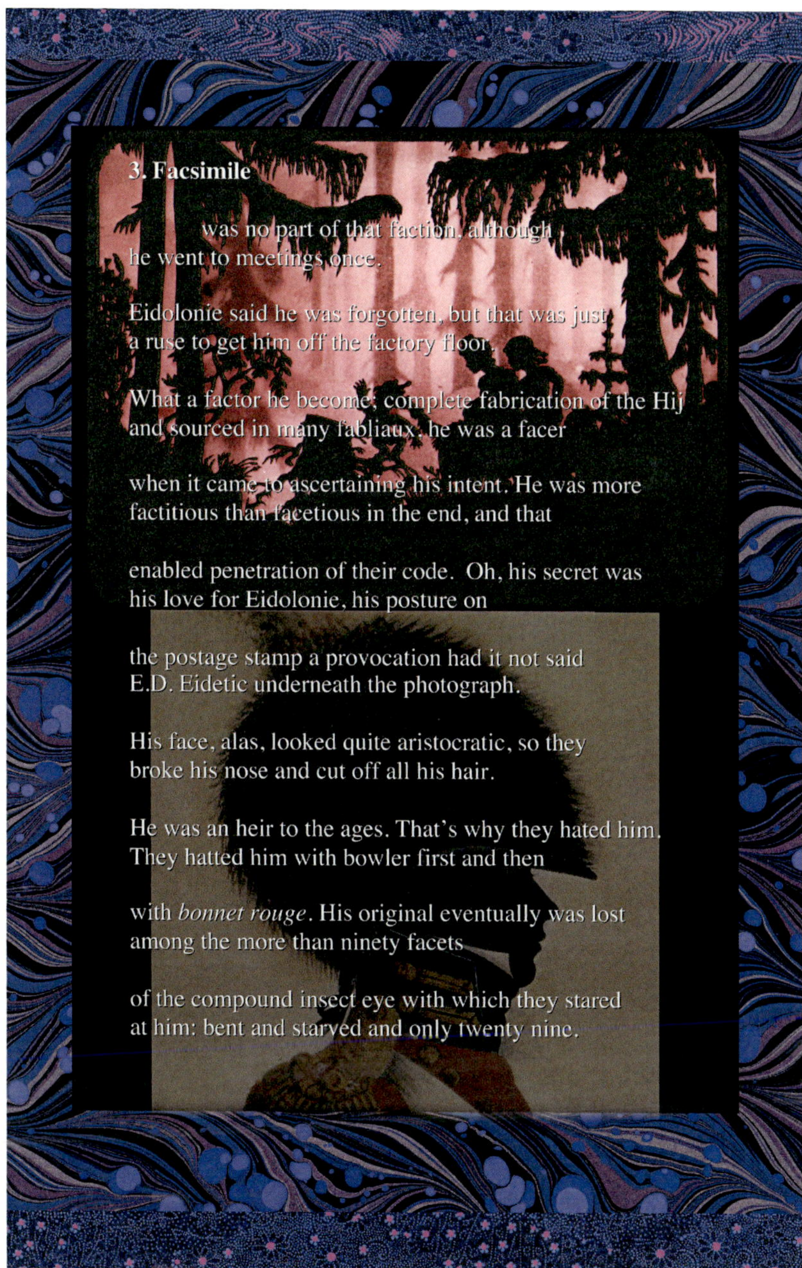

3. Facsimile

       was no part of that faction, although
he went to meetings once.

Eidolonie said he was forgotten, but that was just
a ruse to get him off the factory floor.

What a factor he become; complete fabrication of the Hij
and sourced in many fabliaux, he was a facer

when it came to ascertaining his intent. He was more
factitious than facetious in the end, and that

enabled penetration of their code. Oh, his secret was
his love for Eidolonie, his posture on

the postage stamp a provocation had it not said
E.D. Eidetic underneath the photograph.

His face, alas, looked quite aristocratic, so they
broke his nose and cut off all his hair.

He was an heir to the ages. That's why they hated him.
They hatted him with bowler first and then

with *bonnet rouge*. His original eventually was lost
among the more than ninety facets

of the compound insect eye with which they stared
at him: bent and starved and only twenty nine.

F is for facets in an insect's eye

Literary criticism, hatted first with bowler, then with bonnet rouge, looks at "The HIJ" in more than ninety ommatidial facets of its insect eye, viz.:

Aestheticist (old)
Aestheticist (new)
Allegorical
American pragmatic
Anthropological
Architectonic
Aristotelian (unreconstructed)
Aristotelian (neo-)
Arnoldian
Bakhtinian
Barthesian
Bloomian
Butlerian
Chicago School
Cognitive culturalist
Cognitive neuroscientific
Cognitive evolutionary psychological
Comparative
Culturalist
Cultural Materialist
Dark Ecological
Darwinian
Deconstructivist
Deleuzian
Diacritical
Digital Humanistic
Eco-Critical
Ethical

Existentialist
Feminist (first wave)
Feminist (second wave)
Feminist (third wave)
Formalist
Foucauldian
Frankfurt School
Freudian
Gadamerian
Gramscian
Habermasian
Heideggerian
Hermeneutic
Historicist (old)
Historicism (new)
Humanist (old)
Humanist (new)
Idealist
Jamesonian
Jaussian
Jungian
Leavisite
Lacanian
Linguistic
Marcusian
Marxian
Marxian-Humanist
Marxist

Morphological
Mythic
Narratological
New Critical
Object-Oriented
Objective Hermeneutical
Ontological
Philological
Philological (neo-)
Platonic
Platonic (neo-)
Positivist
Postcognitive
Postcolonial
Postmodern
Poststructuralist
Prague Structuralist
Proppian
Psychoanalytic
Queer
Reader Responsive
Russian Formalist
Semiotic
Social Constructivist
Sociological
Syncretistic
Structuralist
Taxonomical
Thomistic
Tartu-Muscavite
Todorovian
Weberian
Yale School
Žižekian

1. Nonentity

> would nonchalantly noodle nomagraphs
of straight and curved where Z squared

was equal to his height times weight plus breath,
a malfeasance of the *prima fascia. Hij*, he'd say,

*You nonpareil, don't call me square Z when
I'm your own nonillionth for the nonce, the best*

damn non sequitur in town. His mother had him
singing l-m-n-o-p when he was two. He asked

her for the "alpaphet song." First she'd sing it,
then he'd have of go. *Enupofit* he'd finally say,

and then she'd mop his drooling gob. The Hij
wiped the floor with him, cleaned his clock,

locked him nightly in the fridge. He couldn't any longer
stand the look of him, and kicked him

with a square boot of ten. *Fuckin' Nopofit you
nonentity,* he'd say. *Now I understand why*

*your mother baked you in a pie. Heave-ho
me ice cube, hot stuff at only two,*

at twenty pretty cool – a nomination to the nines,
nonesuch assassin and the ides a go.

1. Nonentity

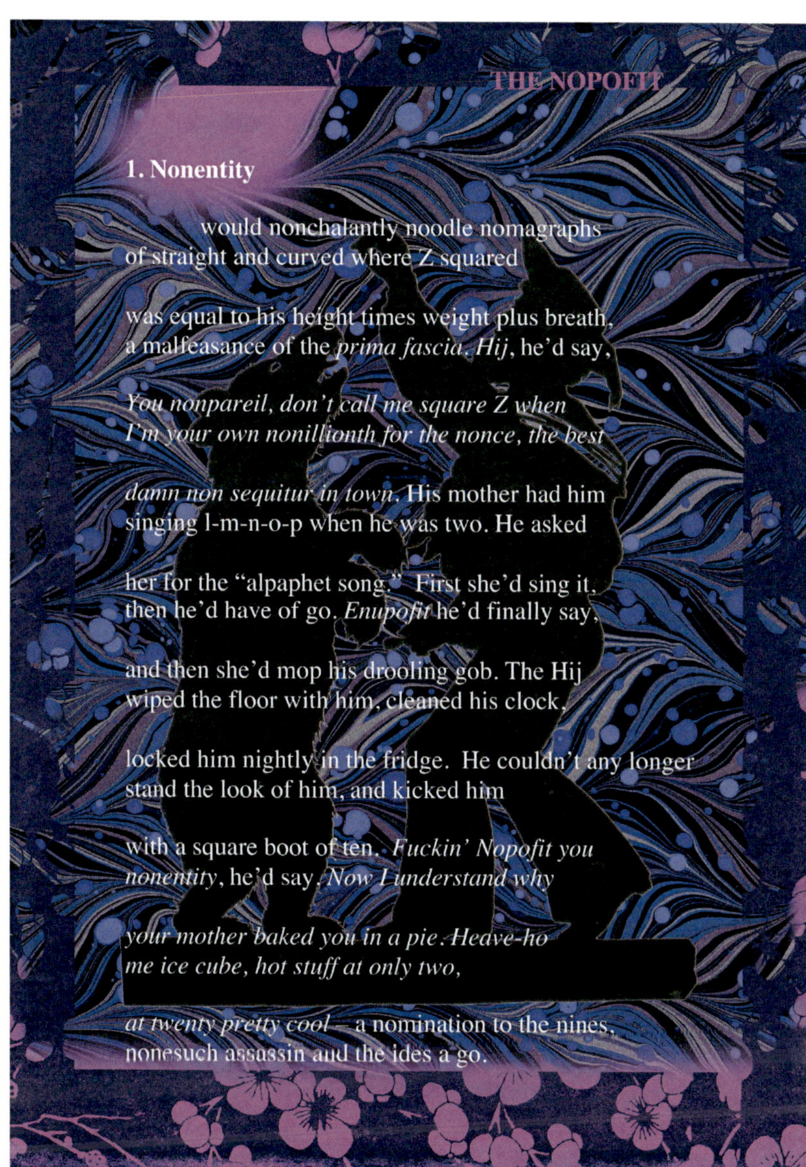

would nonchalantly noodle nomagraphs
of straight and curved where Z squared

was equal to his height times weight plus breath,
a malfeasance of the *prima fascia. Hij*, he'd say,

*You nonpareil, don't call me square Z when
I'm your own nonillionth for the nonce, the best*

damn non sequitur in town. His mother had him
singing l-m-n-o-p when he was two. He asked

her for the "alpaphet song." First she'd sing it,
then he'd have of go. *Enupofit* he'd finally say,

and then she'd mop his drooling gob. The Hij
wiped the floor with him, cleaned his clock,

locked him nightly in the fridge. He couldn't any longer
stand the look of him, and kicked him

with a square boot of ten. *Fuckin' Nopofit you
nonentity*, he'd say. *Now I understand why*

*your mother baked you in a pie. Heave-ho
me ice cube, hot stuff at only two,*

at twenty pretty cool — a nomination to the nines,
nonesuch assassin and the ides a go.

N is for not over yet

"Bucyrus," the title poem of John Matthias' 1970 first book of poems, is strange stuff and might not even be a poem. It is a tale about three aunts who keep two sixteen-year-olds prisoner in their house and force them to recite by rote the tenets of *Dianetics*, the puritanical theology of Richard Baxter, and the rules of Anglo-Saxon grammar. The aunts seek to keep pure a story they relate about their father, Bucyrus, whose disembodied spirit still haunts the house. In the aunts' story, Bucyrus, a middle-aged virgin of set habits, was the victim of Becky, a waitress who invaded his house, cooked for him, raped him nightly, and bore him three daughters before being banished. If Ada and Aben (the adolescents in the aunts' charge) deviate from this story in retelling it, they are punished, as they are if they fail when reciting the rules of Anglo-Saxon grammar or the tenets of Baxter and L. Ron Hubbard. The opening gives a sense of the poem's unusual texture:

> "Don't do that," said Aunt Ooney. "Don't do that," said
> Aunt Olley.
> "Don't do that," said Aunt Oam.
> *Don't do what?* asked the midnight darkness pierced
> by Olley's flashlight beam. *And why not do it?* asked
> Bucyrus, dead Bucyrus, uncle of drawn curtains and
> tar-papered windows. *And why not do it, Aunts?*
> "Your law forbids," said Oam.
> "And Baxter rests," Olley whispered. "He rests ever
> lastingly." "As dianetical truth reveals, " added Ooney.
> "As truth reveals."
> *But don't do what?* asked Bucyrus through the night
> again. *Tell me Aunts of shadows.*
> "Thou shalt not copulate upon the floor at midnight,"
> they all sang. "Up, Aben, Up, Ada. Get up. Thou shalt
> do thy Anglo-Saxon Grammar."

Outside of this world hovers an unknown force, threatening to break into the closed system. This manifests itself via a refrain running through the poem: "Here, there was an insistent, violent knocking at the door." Is this Bucyrus, returning? We never find out—Ada breaks the spell of the aunts by refusing to buy into their stories and language games. She refuses to believe in Becky's malevolence, and in doing so sets herself and her brother free.

Matthias has often distanced himself from "Bucyrus." When it appeared in his 1995 book *Beltane at Aphelion: Collected Longer Poems*, it bore the dedication "For a Class of 1968"—as if Matthias wished to apologize for a youthful indiscretion, or to confine the poem to his past, its authorship to a past self. When Matthias prepared his 2012 Collected Longer Poems for publication, he chose to exclude the poem altogether.

But "Bucyrus" will not stay locked away. "Bucyrus" is omnipresent in Matthias' poetry, its center everywhere, its circumference nowhere. Consider the title character of "Nonentity." Unlike Ada and Aben, he has no domineering aunts who resemble the witch from "Hansel and Gretel," but he does have an overwhelming mother who comes out of the world of fairy tales and nursery rhymes (she baked him in a pie). Nonentity knows nothing of Anglo-Saxon grammar, but he does sing, under this mother's direction, the alphabet song, l-m-n-o-p. Consider, too, the Hij keeping Nonentity as a domestic prisoner, locking him away in the fridge—a confinement not unlike that of Ada and Aben. And consider the role of the alphabet as the generator of the character's names.

Power, sadism, and confinement, connected with the alphabet and arbitrary rules of language—these, and the innocence of the victims, can be found in Matthias' work from nearly a half century ago, and are found here, too. Matthias may wish to be done with "Bucyrus." Maybe he is done with it. But it isn't done with him, not yet. Matthias may want to throw "Bucyrus"—the nullified poem, the nonentity of 2012—into the fridge to cool, but he can't. It wanders outside the house where Matthias mutters his alphabet, hammering to get in.

2. Onomastic

        was a Greek who ran the diner where the Hij
did his deals among Russkies and the Polish bards.

Oneiromancy, one-night-stands, and
one-up-manship were deals. The Greek was meant to

name them but he couldn't find the port of Nakhodka
on the map or part with nabobs in his clientele.

The Hij hedged his bets on ontology and waited
for ontogeny to recapitulate phylogeny. Nabobs didn't

know the difference between *O* and *Oh*, but the onus
was on all the oligarchs who also gathered at

the dining place committing onanistic acts in
coffee cups when O's pretty waitress stripped right down

to bra and little thong and murmured *Oh*!
This gave the Hij an opening to intervene on his ophicleide.

Everyone was so opinionated. *O*! said the Polish master,
baiting Greek and oligarch, Hij and nabob,

nonentity and nonpareil, *Don't you know the difference
between a caught breath of surprise and a long breath*

*of wonder? Nine to twenty are the odds, O my even Ohs,
that it's Aoi or an ogle in your next cynganedd.*

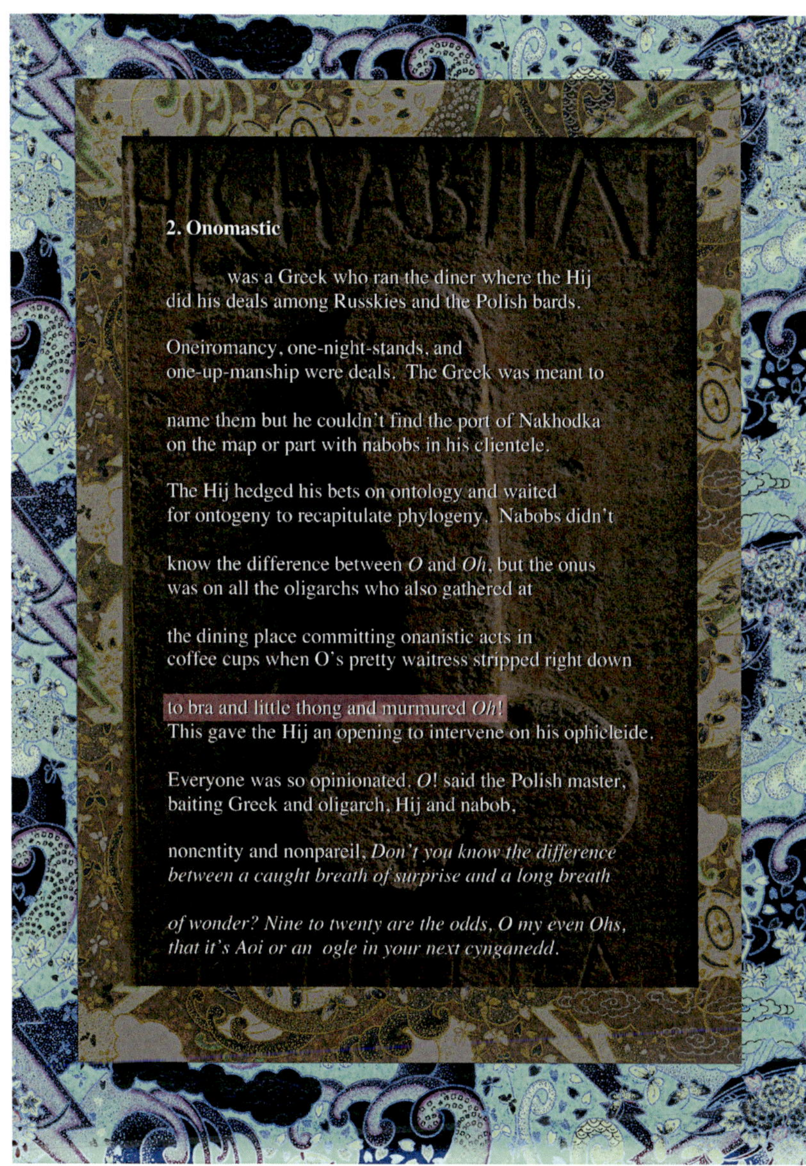

2. Onomastic

       was a Greek who ran the diner where the Hij
did his deals among Russkies and the Polish bards.

Oneiromancy, one-night-stands, and
one-up-manship were deals. The Greek was meant to

name them but he couldn't find the port of Nakhodka
on the map or part with nabobs in his clientele.

The Hij hedged his bets on ontology and waited
for ontogeny to recapitulate phylogeny. Nabobs didn't

know the difference between *O* and *Oh*, but the onus
was on all the oligarchs who also gathered at

the dining place committing onanistic acts in
coffee cups when O's pretty waitress stripped right down

to bra and little thong and murmured *Oh*!
This gave the Hij an opening to intervene on his ophicleide.

Everyone was so opinionated. *O!* said the Polish master,
baiting Greek and oligarch, Hij and nabob,

nonentity and nonpareil, *Don't you know the difference
between a caught breath of surprise and a long breath

of wonder? Nine to twenty are the odds, O my even Ohs,
that it's Aoi or an ogle in your next cynganedd.*

O is for Oulipo

Oulipo—the *Ouvroir de literature potentielle*—isn't dead. Perhaps this would surprise Raymond Queneau and François Le Lionnais, who founded the movement in 1960. What avant-gardeist would dream of durability, when the ephemeral is so often the nature of their tradition? The professors and pataphysicians who founded the movement have all passed from this earth, but many of their anointed heirs remain, and continue the Oulipan mode of writing under the inspiration of artificial constraints (George Perec's *La disparition,* a novel-length lipogram, written without the use of the letter 'e' remains the greatest monument of the movement).

But it isn't just the anointed who inherit: consider Christian Bök. His Eunoia may be the most thoroughly Oulipan work of our current century. A standard reference work gives a sense of the constraints under which Bök chooses to labor:

> The main section of the book consists of five chap ters: "A", "E", "I", "O" and "U". In each of these chapters, the only vowel used is the same one as the title. For example, in Chapter A, the only vowel used is "A". There are other rules given to each of the chapters. Each of the chapters must refer to the art of writing. Each of the chapters has "to describe a culinary banquet, a prurient debauch, a pastoral tableau and a nautical voyage." All the sentences must have an "accented internal rhyme through the use of syntactical parallelism." The text must include as many words as possible. The postscript of the book says that each chapter uses at least 98% of the available words. The text must avoid repeating words as much as possible. The letter "Y" is unused. The chap ters are dedicated to Hans Arp, René Crevel, Dick Higgins, Yoko Ono, and Zhu Yu, respectively.

If there is an opposite to automatic writing, it is this—unless, of course, we see the system of constraints as a machine automatically generating text, as well we might.

But what of Matthias? Does his "The HIJ" inherit from the Oulipans? Certainly he has chosen his constraints. They are nine and twenty. That is: not 29 constraints (a number to balk even Bök). But twenty lines per section as an arbitrary length, and the first nine-letter words he finds in his dictionary for each of his title letters—from H to J, from D to F, from N to P. So here: "onomastic," "oligarchs," and "onanistic." He slips the cuffs of his constraints and indulges himself with adjacent words that catch his eye: "oneiromancy" and "ogle," "ontogeny" and "opinionated," "ophicleide" and "onus," "O" and "Oh." The chosen constraint, the dictionary, and the browser's roving eye are the arbitrary generators of material, shaped by the poet who willingly takes the gamble he'll be able to make it work. *"Nine to twenty are the odds, O my even Ohs."*

The constraints of nine and twenty are only the crudest of Matthias' principles of generation, though. "The HIJ" involves an array of means for deriving text from text, well beyond the dictionary. There are words generated from other words by virtue of the resemblance of sound to sound (a technique as old as poetry). There are mutations and recombinations of events, characters, and images. While Matthias' penchant for allusions to history, especially aesthetic history, will always tie him to Pound, there is a sense in which "The HIJ" starts to resemble another branch of Modernism, that for which Gertrude Stein is the exemplary figure. Language starts to take its primary cue from language, rather than reference, and the narrative in "The HIJ" starts to take on the qualities of shattered or obscured reference we see in "Tender Buttons." Which is to say: the referent appears in "The HIJ" much as the guitar or vase appears in the early Cubist work of Braque or

Picasso. It peeks out from behind a scrim of angles and formal obstruction. We can see it neither steadily nor whole.

You might well ask why. I can only speculate—and I will. The journey from communicative reference to the foregrounding of language itself is a journey into autonomy: into those things that a poet has to himself, as his domain. The poet decides to work with various words not because they connect directly to the world around him, but because they connect to the array of language he has established as his domain in writing. This domain is removed, by one or more levels of mediation, from the world where words seek only to have consequence. It is a mud hut for hermits, perhaps for holy men. In a wounding world it returns poets to a throne they know to be their own. It is a golden fleece.

Critics go there too.

3. Plastered

          in their local and unlikely Jerkwater pub,
Facsimile, Nonentity, Haphazard, and the Hij

continued buying one another pints.
They'd moved on from the greasy Grecian spoon

once they heard that Planck (Max) was constant
and Plantagenet out at their plantation.

Gypsum cement, hemi-hydrated cal of sulfate, all
were plantigrade of foot when not plangent otherwise

On ophicleides or circulating in the planetary nebula.
The Hij thought he was immortal as the Pleiades

but still was enamored of the Eidolon whose lover he
had lofted to the Eigon Alp. Poor old good old Hij.

Ahpf! Borsht! He missed his sentimental meetings with
The Bishop of Pah. *Jerkwater's the limit,* he was

heard to say. *Thank you Jeroboam. I may be a plaster cast
but I am still the boss. Bastard of a plasmagene at payoff,*

*I'm also Pliny with a pistol on a plinth. Evolved from
the Pliocene, I am here to stay.*

*Measure me a nine-and-twenty, plimsolls off in May:
Dummkopffts on double-docket, dizened for today.*

3. Plastered

          in their local and unlikely Jerkwater pub,
Facsimile, Nonentity, Haphazard, and the Hij

continued buying one another pints.
They'd moved on from the greasy Grecian spoon

once they heard that Planck (Max) was constant
and Plantagenet out at their plantation.

Gypsum cement, hemi-hydrated cal of sulfate, all
were plantigrade of foot when not plangent otherwise

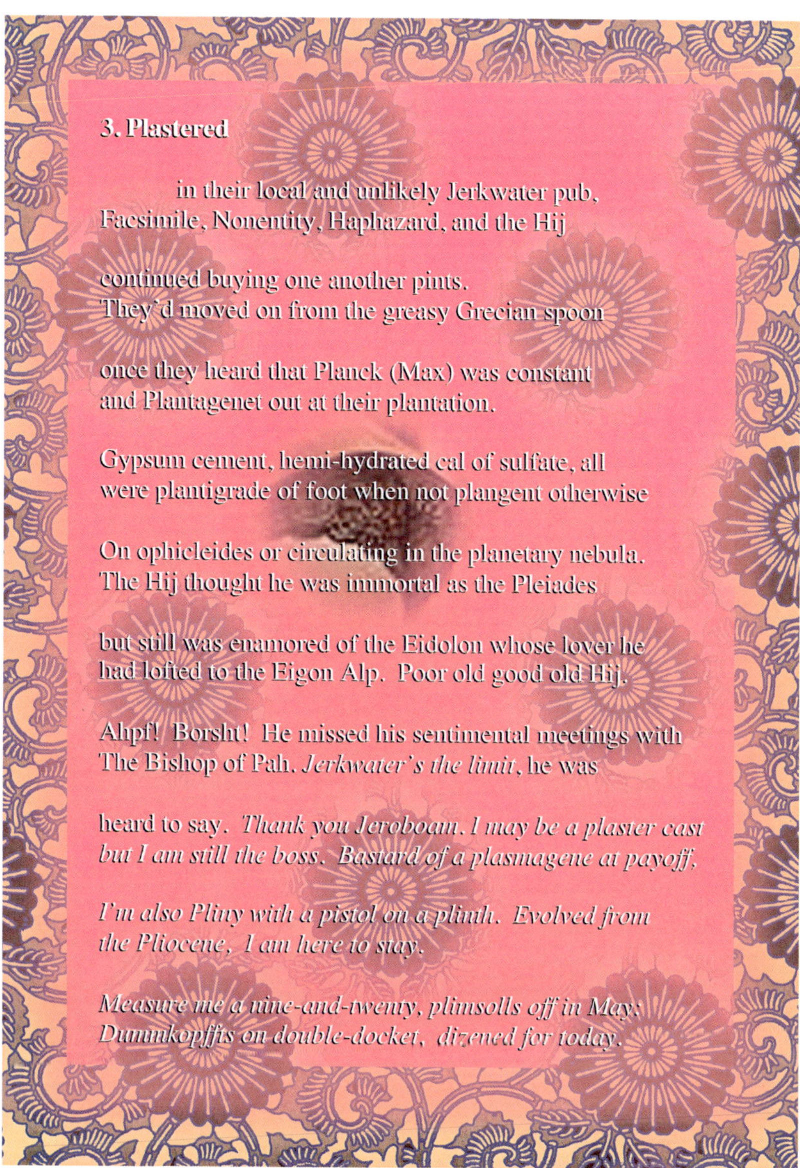

On ophicleides or circulating in the planetary nebula.
The Hij thought he was immortal as the Pleiades

but still was enamored of the Eidolon whose lover he
had lofted to the Eigon Alp. Poor old good old Hij.

Ahpf! Borsht! He missed his sentimental meetings with
The Bishop of Pah. *Jerkwater's the limit*, he was

heard to say. *Thank you Jeroboam. I may be a plaster cast
but I am still the boss. Bastard of a plasmagene at payoff,*

*I'm also Pliny with a pistol on a plinth. Evolved from
the Pliocene, I am here to stay.*

*Measure me a nine-and-twenty, plimsolls off in May;
Dummkopffis on double-docket, dizened for today.*

P becomes D, and D is for dizen

We end with "Dummkopffts on double-docket, dizened for today." We know dummkopffts, all of us (alas). We know the docket. But dizened? From "distaff," the cleft pole from which hung the thread, waiting to be spun. An older form of "bedizen," meaning to dress or adorn in a gaudy manner. So Hawthorne, in *The Scarlet Letter*: "Prithee, young one, who art thou, and what has ailed thy mother to bedizen thee in this strange fashion?"

And what has Matthias done but dizen his dictionary? What has he done but hang fleece from the dizened distaff, weave it, and try to dye it gold? What ailed him to bedizen words in this strange fashion? What fleece is gold, and what's it for?

*

Vincent Sherry, on Matthias' dizening:

On the one hand, Matthias the pedagogue offers from his word-hoard and reference trove the splen did alterity of unfamiliar speech; on the other, this is our familial tongue, our own language in its deeper memory and reference. It is strange only in the ways of the uncanny or, more suitably, the *unheimlich*, in the double implication of the German word's literal and Freudian meanings: not homey or not familiar but only because too intimate and well known, and strange only because repressed, or forgotten. This is the paradox that defines the enlivening conflict of Matthias' verse. Here is a poet who must work, as it were, way out in the center. He is an idiosyncratic radical who is only trying to get back to a common root . . . aiming to reclaim and consolidate a language that is already there, the true depth of our civil speech.

*

Dizen: in Spanish, "they say," sometimes used as a veiled way of attributing information to a source (the usage occurs twice, for example, in the prosification of the first canto of *The Poem of The Cid*, both times with reference to obscure omens). The term is also Ladino, and used to great effect in the poetry of Bouena Sarfatty, verse chronicler of the embattled Sephardic community in Nazi occupied Greece.

> *Ounos dizen me flato; otros dizen me dio enchavonada.*
> *Ounos dizen se arezvalo, otros dizen se mourio.*
> *Ounos dizen kayadez, otros dizen amoudesian.*
> *Bevamos a la saloud de Avraam Sion.*

> Some say he flattered me; others say he pulled the
>   wool over my eyes.
> Some say he slipped away; others say he died.
> Some say be quiet; other say shut up.
> Let us drink to the health of Avraham Sion.

Though few know it, the Hij would go by the name of Avraham Sion, dizen himself, when convenient, with that grand and resonant name. Some call the Hij a flatterer, some say he pulls the wool over our eyes. Some say he's slipped away, some say he died. He will be quiet, now, oh yes. He will shut up.

Let us drink to his health. Hoist high a glass. Bedizened, begotten, be given, be gone. The Hij, the Hij, the Hij.

Epilogue: The Hij's Happy Book of Insults

you're a Hindoo Haji Hoky Half-Cast Hun you Hippie
Hymie Jerry Jocky Kaffir Katsap Jigaboo

[big breath]

You Limey Lace Curtain Irish Mickey Mammy Moskal
Nig-nog Nip you Pakki Pancake Pepper

[breath]

Poncho Polack Pom you Redneck Redskin Sasquatch
Sambo Shiksa Skippy Slopehead Southern Fairy

[breath]

Spearchucker Taffy Tinker Towelheadded Uncle Tom
You Wog you Wap Albino Abbo Alligator bait

[breath]

You Ape you Argie Beaner Boche you Bog Irish Bohunk
Camel Jocky Charlie Chee-chee Chinaman

[breath]

You Cholo Coolie Coconut you Cunt-eyed Cracker Crow you
Jigarooni Dhoti Dink you Dutchman Eskimo you FreeState Flipnit

Greaseball Gringo Gypsy Beatnik Guido Gimp you

You . . . You . . .
Yoyo   Yankeedoodle Jingo Jerk

You Wetback Anchorbaby Gimcrack Mayflower Mug

you're a Hindoo Haji Hoky Half-Cast Hun you Hippie
Hymie Jerry Jocky Kaffir Katsap Jigaboo

[big breath]

You Limey Lace Curtain Irish Mickey Mammy Moskal
Nig-nog Nip you Pakki Pancake Pepper

[breath]

Poncho Polack Pom you Redneck Redskin Sasquatch
Sambo Shiksa Skippy Slopehead Southern Fairy

[breath]

Spearchucker Taffy Tinker Towelheadded Uncle Tom
You Wog you Wap Albino Abbo Alligator bait

[breath]

You Ape you Argie Beaner Boche you Bog Irish Bohunk
Camel Jocky Charlie Chee-chee Chinaman

[breath]

You Cholo Coolie Coconut you Cunt-eyed Cracker Crow you
Jigarooni Dhoti Dink you Dutchman Eskimo you FreeState Flipnit

Greaseball Gringo Gypsy Beatnik Guido Gimp you

You . . . You . . .
Yoyo   Yankeedoodle Jingo Jerk

You Wetback Anchorbaby Gimcrack Mayflower Mug

51

After the Epilogue

No comment

Osip Mandelstam

After Five Words Englished from the Russian

I

Horseshoe or dingbat, Sir   oh just the one
he thought, even if a hoarsepshaw brief Cyrillic Ж was altogether
confidential then. Sadistic counsel goofy as it was to hit
a mark an iron-shod method like an actor on the methadone
for bad habits, pitching his good luck
to brain the brain-damaged boy, altogether his intention
Master Craft, I swear
                    swore it when he outran a goddamn dawn
a good man reigning through obsessive thought that inning out to bean
him break his neck   Focus on the other's head
a dingbat or lucky shot   pitching high and inside
fucking up the outdoors, even fireworks on the Fourth   can't you
do an elementary task?
                    However,
He Who Finds a Horseshoe fires a synapse begs a question
but in time bags his quarry by the marsh
even brags about it, flees as far as Moony Lake running
in the tallest grass and crouching down they say
it's possible to drown in mud and sand and shoreline
stagnant pools in short order, Sir.
I Babel's unit, Blogmeister Ulyanov. A thrice- beaten hoarse
without a pshaw is very dark indeed.

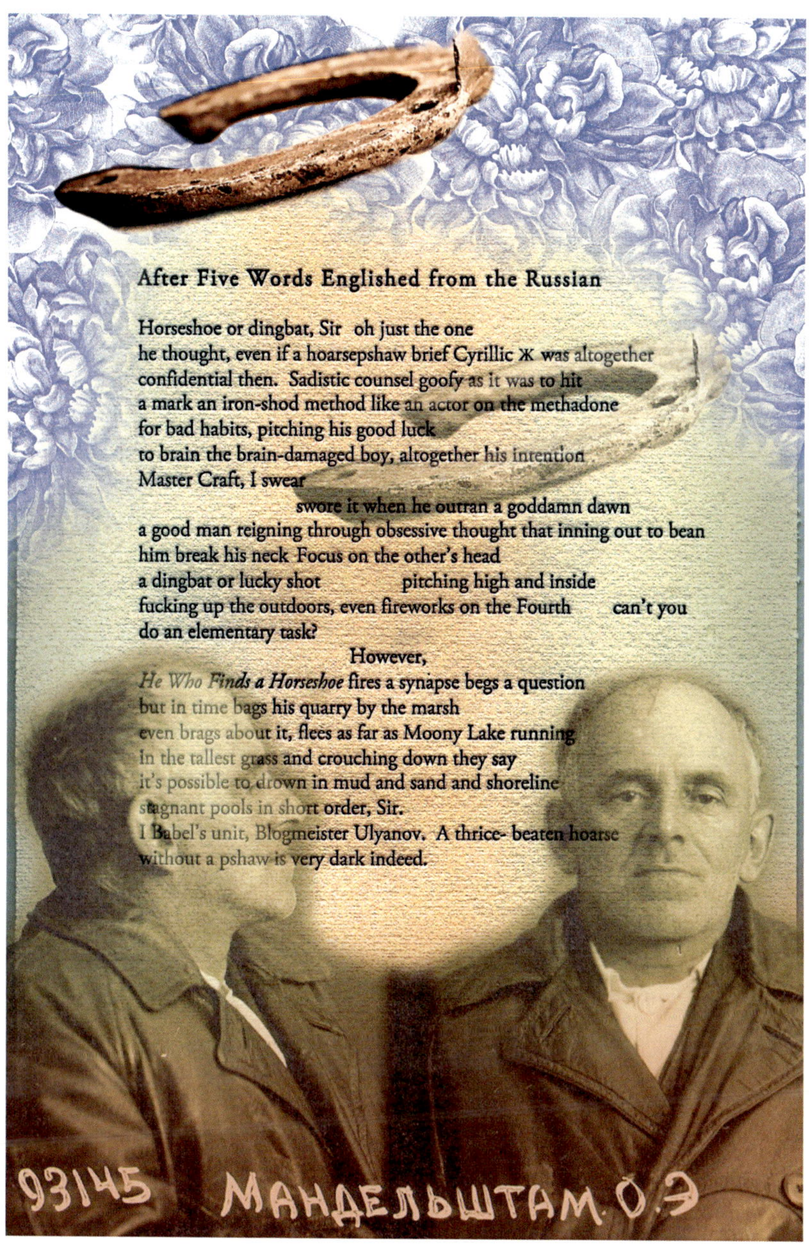

After Five Words Englished from the Russian

Horseshoe or dingbat, Sir oh just the one
he thought, even if a hoarsepshaw brief Cyrillic Ж was altogether
confidential then. Sadistic counsel goofy as it was to hit
a mark an iron-shod method like an actor on the methadone
for bad habits, pitching his good luck
to brain the brain-damaged boy, altogether his intention
Master Craft, I swear
                swore it when he outran a goddamn dawn
a good man reigning through obsessive thought that inning out to bean
him break his neck Focus on the other's head
a dingbat or lucky shot   pitching high and inside
fucking up the outdoors, even fireworks on the Fourth   can't you
do an elementary task?
              However,
He Who Finds a Horseshoe fires a synapse begs a question
but in time bags his quarry by the marsh
even brags about it, flees as far as Moony Lake running
in the tallest grass and crouching down they say
it's possible to drown in mud and sand and shoreline
stagnant pools in short order, Sir.
I Babel's unit, Blogmeister Ulyanov. A thrice- beaten hoarse
without a pshaw is very dark indeed.

He is Mandelstam

"Sometimes," wrote Osip Mandelstam, "air is dark, like water, and everything living/Swims in it like a fish." That was in 1923, in the poem "He Who Finds A Horseshoe." He'd been married for a year or so, to Nadezhda, though he still chased other women—desire alive all around him, he swam in it, a shark surrounded by a thousand tempting fish. He worried, often, about what could last—the last Tsar dead, the world shaken by war, his faithlessness a threat to those he loved. In his poem he imagines a man who finds a horseshoe and, lifting it up, hangs it above a door:

> He who finds a horseshoe
> Blows the dust from it
> And polishes it with wool
> till it gleams.
> Then
> He hangs it upon the doorway,
> So that it may rest,
> And for it there will be no more striking
> sparks from the flint.

Up from the world of decay, out of the world of use, it becomes something else—an aesthetic object, perhaps. And it endures.

Or, rather: it endures for a while. Mandelstam goes on to describe coins taken from the earth, each with the emblem of some forgotten time, some long-gone regime—a head, a lion—each worn in its own way ("their centuries leave/upon them an imprint like teeth"). None of these recovered relics endures undamaged or forever. Like the horseshoe over the door, they are still in the flux of time, will suffer new wounds, will be trimmed away, taking on a different kind of beauty before disappearing again, eventually for good. In this, says Mandelstam, they are like people, like poems, like Mandelstam himself—"Time clips my edges, like a silver penny," he writes, "And I no longer have enough of myself."

The five words Matthias sees Englished from the Russian are the words of Mandelstam's title—"He Who Finds a Horseshoe." Matthias' horseshoes are American, Midwestern, even—one sees them pitched through the air on a summer night, a lawn game meant to lift us up from the world of work, of use, and into the realm of play—that most sacred realm for Matthias; that most redemptive world in all his work—if "work" is the word we want, which it decidedly is not.

He gives us a summer camp, a world that's meant for play. But his camp's no good: the counselor is sadistic, shouting cruelly at a fumbling child ("can't you/do an elementary task?"). And the innocent game of horseshoes? It can hurt. That iron in the air comes down, and can brain an errant boy.

The real menace of Matthias' camp isn't the counselor, or the horseshoes in the air: it's something heard in the echo. His poem comes from Mandelstam's, and Mandelstam would meet a real shark a decade after he wrote of horseshoes on the wall. He'd write "The Kremlin Mountaineer," and even though he read it only to a trusted few, the word got out: he'd written against Stalin. His fate was clear: he was for the Gulag, for the camps. He disappeared.

And what endures? The horseshoe of his poem, sure. For now, for us. And in Matthias' poem, Mandelstam is everywhere. His notion of what endures itself endures, gets marked by time, a century's new imprint on its surface. And what mark does Matthias make on Mandelstam's coin? He stamps it with a new anxiety, the loss of memory (he'd seen dementia in his parents, he'd watched his wife's memories begin to slip away). He'd worried about what would last. He'd thought of his past, of running out to Mooney Lake. He finds a Russian horseshoe and polishes it with wool until it gleams.

In the long run in short it was like this: He stumbled bleeding
into foreign camp where all the officers played
dice with nasty dingbats, bits of backbone lacking, they main-
tained, in cowards who'd run off. Their poet said that what he
said was never said by him. But also *Three times blessed is one
who puts a name in song.* Mandelstam. Ulyanov. Babel:
*No iron can pierce the human heart with the force of a period just
exactly in the right place*

Aplysia at just that point in time became, like injured campers,
Useful slugs in neurobiological associative tasks.
Aplasia, though, prevented both the classical and operant con-
ditioning.

Iron bomb's your balalaika too? And you an anarchist like me?
In this day and age, the pleaЖure is entirely mine.

In the long run in short it was like this: He stumbled bleeding
into foreign camp where all the officers played
dice with nasty dingbats, bits of backbone lacking, they maintained,
in cowards who'd run off. Their poet said that what he said
was never said by him. But also *Three times blessed is one who
puts a name in song*. Mandelstam. Ulyanov. Babel:
*No iron can pierce the human heart with the force of a period just
exactly in the right place*

Aplysia at just that point in time became, like injured campers,
Useful slugs in neurobiological associative tasks.
Aplasia, though, prevented both the classical and operant conditioning.

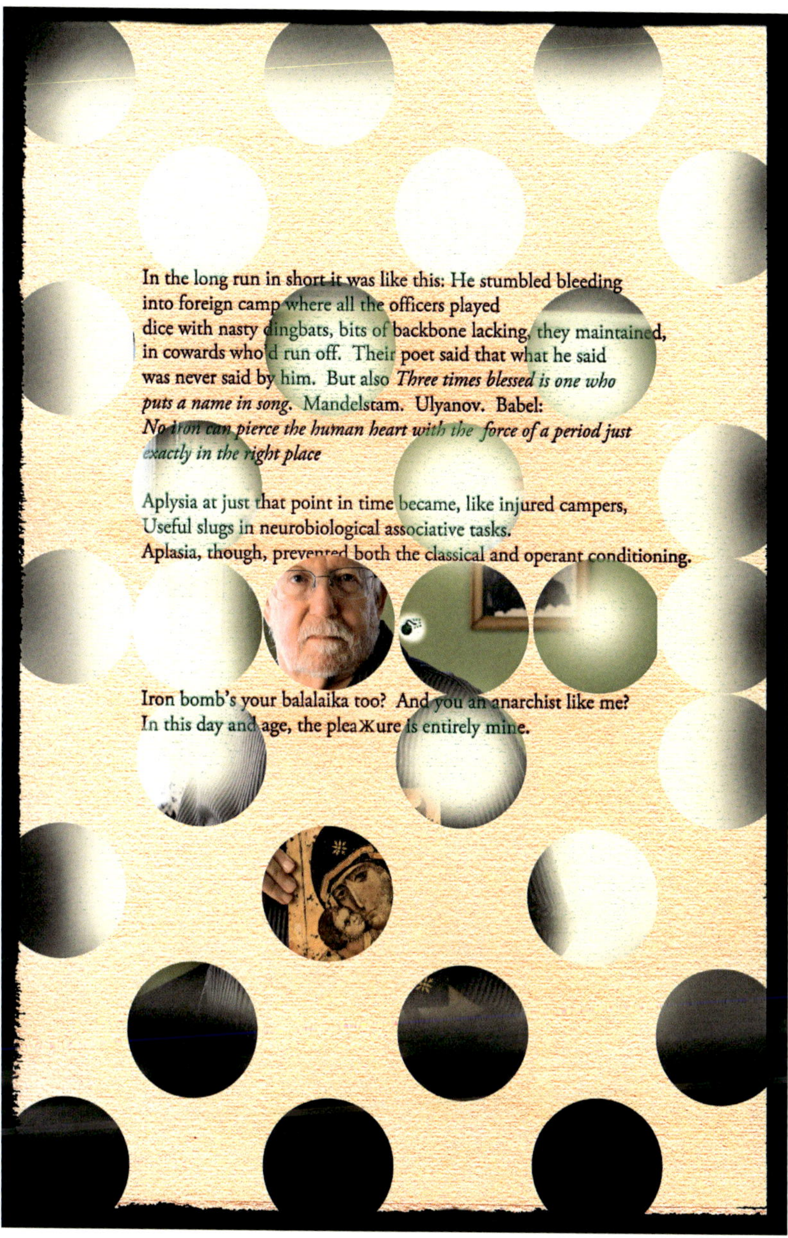

Iron bomb's your balalaika too? And you an anarchist like me?
In this day and age, the pleaЖure is entirely mine.

Who is not a proper name?

"Three times blessed is one who puts a name in song," said Mandelstam, whose name recurs many times in Matthias' poem. But how many times blessed is one who puts 1500 names in a song? That, after all, is the number of the instances of proper names in John Matthias' cycle of longer poems *A Gathering of Ways*. Those names, Brooke Bergan writes, belong to people known and obscure, gods celebrated and lost, saints canonical and heretical, to:

> …churches and abbeys, paintings and painters, songs and their singers, chronicles and their chroniclers, ships, cars, constellations, rivers, lakes, mountains, mounds, roads and the towns they lead to, nations and the battlefields that created them. There are nicknames (El Cid, from *as-sid,* Mozarabic for *lord*), surnames (Cooper, Joliet, Picaud), fictional names (pseudo-Turpin), and mythological ones (Wiske), and names that are both (Terpsichore, the ship and the muse; Roland, and the actual Turpin, who appears in *The Song of Roland* but was apparently miles from the actual battle). There are eponyms like "the Studebaker/& the Bendix," anachronisms like "the Frankish Blitzkrieg," acronyms like "E.T.A.," and adjectives "Devonion and Trenton." Perhaps most fascinating are the names that are never named or are named belatedly.

Let no one say Matthias doesn't love a name: he generates great clouds of them in poems. And here he gives us three. The first is Mandelstam's, and one sees why: he's a figure of imagination caught in a world of power, a world that his words escape, but where he disappears. This kind of ambiguous triumph of imagination goes deep in Matthias' work, all the way back to his juvenilia. Or deeper still: to his over-attachment to childhood play, outside the house where his father, the judge, brooded over the fate of other men.

One understands the second named here, too: Isaac Babel. Associated with Mandelstam by nationality and by the grim experience of Russian history in the twentieth century, he is associated phonologically with the idea of the derangement of language. And derangement of language accompanies us throughout "After Five Words Englished from the Russian," a poem whose very title ties us to the many-tongued world we live in since the Tower of Babel's collapse.

But what of the other, Ulyanov? Ulyanov is power itself, but power approached sideways. Ulyanov, after all, is the surname of the man whom the world would know as Lenin, once his pen name pushed his birth name to the footnotes. But could the user of this name be blessed? Isn't his name a curse, set next to the martyred Mandelstam's? Not if we think of memory as sacred. Not if we think of Mandelstam's horseshoe nailed to a wall as an act of preservation in a world of flux, erasure, and destruction. Not if any name in a poem is a horseshoe nailed to a wall.

Should we, though? Should we think of memory as sacred? Matthias asks us to, or almost. We see this because there are not three names in this passage, but five: Mandelstam; Babel; Ulyanov, yes—but also Aplysia and Aplasia. The first is a large marine gastropod, a slug of sorts, sometimes called a sea hare—of little use to you or me, but a special prize to neuroscientists. They find, in its neural structure, keys to understanding the formation of long-term memory. And the near-homonym Aplasia? A word for the failure or cessation of normal regenerative processes. When our memories begin to go, Aplasia has come. The heroes of neuroscience seek in Aplysia a solution to our tragic Aplasia. That is their hope for horseshoes on the wall.

It is worth considering that the Aplysia, when threatened or afraid, releases clouds of ink. Some find the swirling patterns they make in the water beautiful, though the motive force behind them is escape.

II

& shhhhhhh . . . sashays to Жay . . . & does shay &
No iron can pierce and so on just a way of betting on the
pen that's mightier than the sword? You think
that babble saved him. All that playing Cossacks was
to chess what Checka was to his submerged cliché:
No one gets the period in the right place. Full stop, Bakunin.
A friend of ours saw him finger-fucking the countess, then
went off to a commune called K' Klarity. Stammered it so
long ago at Horseshoe Camp they only managed checkers,
chests puffed up by golly nonetheless in pride. And no!
Not a commune merely but a country: It's Charity.

And that's a virtue too, Great Aunt Calamity: tell me Muse
what E flat played as an harmonic on a single string
can say to the amped-up soundtrack rocking the whole square
until the child screams and holds his ears and Dingbat's
prancing Lipizzaner slips on the cobbled street and breaks a leg.
Then you must put him down. A mistake: They pitched
their good luck then and brained the brain-damaged boy.
All that rock n' roll at such a volume it would surely damage
anybody's brain. Had you been at the May parade, it would
have damaged yours. Even had you volunteered as number
one sadistic counselor. After all, it was a job.

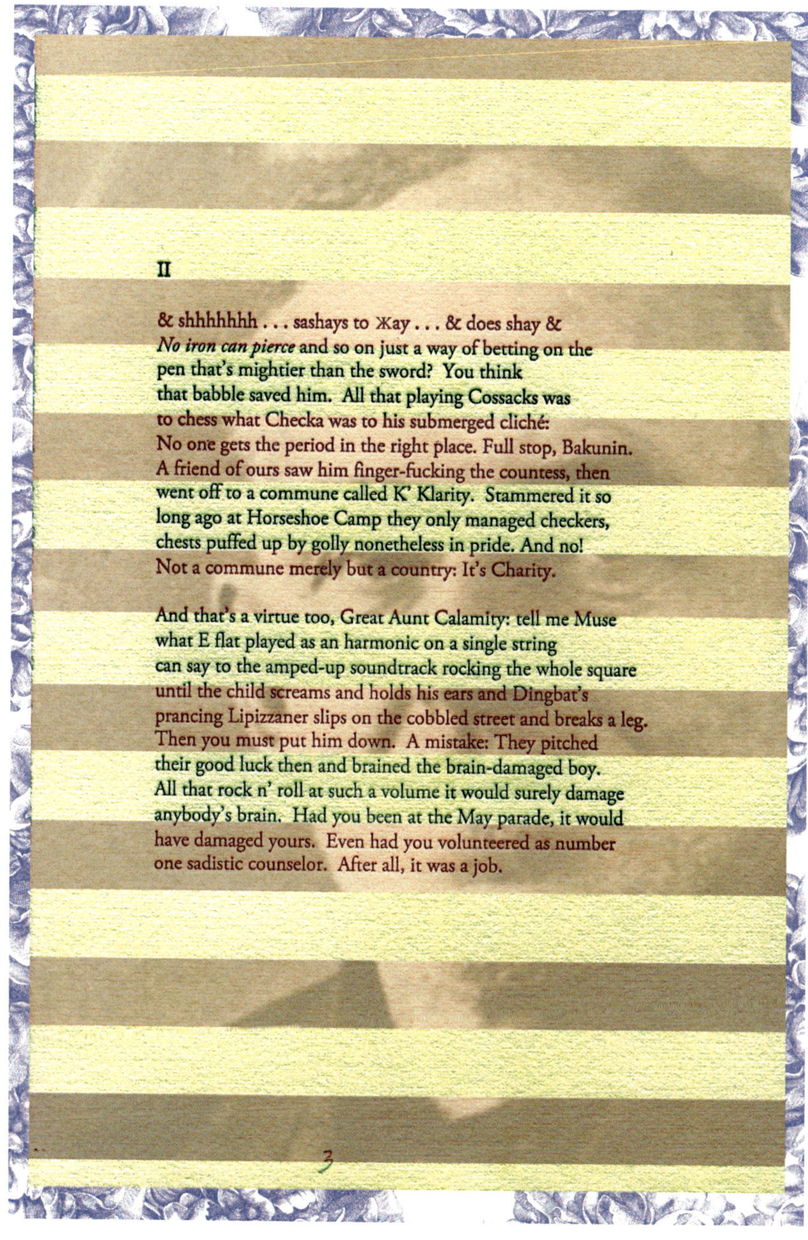

II

& shhhhhhh . . . sashays to Жаy . . . & does shay &
No iron can pierce and so on just a way of betting on the
pen that's mightier than the sword? You think
that babble saved him. All that playing Cossacks was
to chess what Checka was to his submerged cliché:
No one gets the period in the right place. Full stop, Bakunin.
A friend of ours saw him finger-fucking the countess, then
went off to a commune called K' Klarity. Stammered it so
long ago at Horseshoe Camp they only managed checkers,
chests puffed up by golly nonetheless in pride. And no!
Not a commune merely but a country: It's Charity.

And that's a virtue too, Great Aunt Calamity: tell me Muse
what E flat played as an harmonic on a single string
can say to the amped-up soundtrack rocking the whole square
until the child screams and holds his ears and Dingbat's
prancing Lipizzaner slips on the cobbled street and breaks a leg.
Then you must put him down. A mistake: They pitched
their good luck then and brained the brain-damaged boy.
All that rock n' roll at such a volume it would surely damage
anybody's brain. Had you been at the May parade, it would
have damaged yours. Even had you volunteered as number
one sadistic counselor. After all, it was a job.

Finds is a plural noun

        Mandelstam finds a horseshoe, sure, buried in the hardened winter earth of Russia—but his real find came from old Italy: his real find was Dante, whose *Divine Comedy* seemed to him the center and fount of European literature. And Matthias? He finds Mandelstam. He finds him and finds him again, digging up the old Russian horseshoe at unexpected moments throughout his poetic career, from the early "Nightmare After Mandelstam" (he feared the Chicago cops as Mandelstam feared the NKVD), in "Horace Augustus Mandelstam Stalin" (oh poetry, oh power, oh pain); in "Sadnesses: Black Sea" (Matthias knew a thing about exile, albeit internal, albeit in South Bend); in "For John, After His Visit, Suffolk, Fall" (at war with institutions); in "The Memoirists" (memory, again); in the "Aruski Rehab" parts of *Trigons* (writing on others writing on the writing of the dead).

        To join these finds, my own. Found online, while looking for Mandelstam's essay on Dante—a study guide to the essay itself, "Conversation About Dante":

        Mandelstam, in fact, proclaimed that for him Dante was the supreme, indeed, the 'ideal' poet. The Italian was a writer and social outcast whose life was rooted in cultural history. Yet he was not merely the critical intellectual implied by too literal a translation of the term *raznochinets* from the Russian—a variation of which Mandelstam had even applied to himself as a young poet. Far more than that, Dante, in his estimate, was a 'reader and interpreter of poetry' through whom poetry could at last be perceived as something more than so many tropes, or figurative expressions. It could be grasped in its intellectual, symbolic, and emotional dimensions as 'performance.' Thus, Mandelstam chose

Dante as the theme of his conversation not because he wanted to use him to stimulate an interest in classical studies or to place him in some pantheon for comparison with other great writers. Rather, he chose him simply because he was, in his estimate, the 'unrivaled master of transmutable and convertible poetic material.'

Mandelstam's 'Conversation About Dante' was not intended to be readily understood outside accomplished literary circles. It challenges the reader, as do all Mandelstam's writings, with dozens of historical allusions, with animadversions to his beloved Greek and Roman myths, and with both direct and oblique references to major literary figures of the past—most notably nineteenth and early twentieth century Russian poets. Like an archaeological dig, the essay has many levels that still reinforce one's basic understanding of the culture, and thus the message, being examined.

Essentially an analysis of the nature of poetry, 'Conversation About Dante' explains its hybrid character by constantly referring to Dante as the grand strategist of poetic transmutation and hybridization.

And speaking of transmutation: take this find, and make it new. For "Dante" read "Mandelstam." For "Mandelstam read "Matthias." Allow for a few further mutations, and read it all again:

Matthias, in fact, proclaimed that for him Mandelstam was the supreme, indeed, the 'ideal' poet. The Russian was a writer and social outcast whose life was rooted in cultural history. Yet he was not merely the critical intellectual implied by too literal a translation of the term *raznochinets* from the Russian—a variation of which Matthias had even applied to himself as a young poet (see, for example, "Turns"). Far more than that, Mandelstam, in his estimate, was a 'reader and interpreter of poetry' through whom poetry could at last be perceived as something more than so many tropes, or figurative expressions. It could be grasped in its intellectual, symbolic, and emotional dimensions as 'performance.' Thus, Matthias chose Mandelstam as the theme of his conversation not because he wanted to use him to stimulate an interest in Slavic studies or to place him in some pantheon for comparison with other great writers. Rather, he chose him simply because he was, in his estimate, the 'unrivaled master of transmutable and convertible poetic material.'

Matthias's 'After Five Words Englished From the Russian' was not intended to be readily understood outside accomplished literary circles. It challenges the reader, as do all Matthias's writings, with dozens of historical allusions, with animadversions to his beloved poetic and political biographies, and with both direct and oblique references to major literary figures of the past—most notably nineteenth and early twentieth century Modernist poets. Like an archaeological dig, the poem has many levels that still reinforce one's basic understanding of the culture, and thus the message, being examined.

Essentially an analysis of the nature of poetry, 'After Five Words Englished From the Russian' explains its hybrid character by constantly referring to Mandelstam as the grand strategist of poetic transmutation and hybridization.

These paragraphs are my horseshoes. I hang them here.

So too the bold advance of Ivan Chesnokov right up to
the gates of Chugunov with his regiment of cavalry. They asked
him could he read and write, and could he maybe put some
order in the Orders of the Day. He took his rimless glasses
from his pocket, but did not dismount. What he did
was read aloud the leud jokes told at the Second Congress
of the Comintern. A kind of poetry in that. A kind of horseshoe
thrown with malice at the eyes, the mouth, the balls.
Cousin Klarity, I was only at a camp but you were in camp a.
Rabbi Mordecai was putting into verse the harsh sayings
of the one from Dobryvodka called Inert.

Person of the book, Bookie of the Downbeat. Dingbats all in order
for an answer to the ringing red & black phones.

So too the bold advance of Ivan Chesnokov right up to
the gates of Chugunov with his regiment of cavalry. They asked
him could he read and write, and could he maybe put some
order in the Orders of the Day. He took his rimless glasses
from his pocket, but did not dismount. What he did
was read aloud the leud jokes told at the Second Congress
of the Comintern. A kind of poetry in that. A kind of horseshoe
thrown with malice at the eyes, the mouth, the balls.
Cousin Klarity, I was only at a camp but you were in camp a.
Rabbi Mordecai was putting into verse the harsh sayings
of the one from Dobryvodka called Inert.

📖

Person of the book, Bookie of the Downbeat. Dingbats all in order
for an answer to the ringing red & black phones.

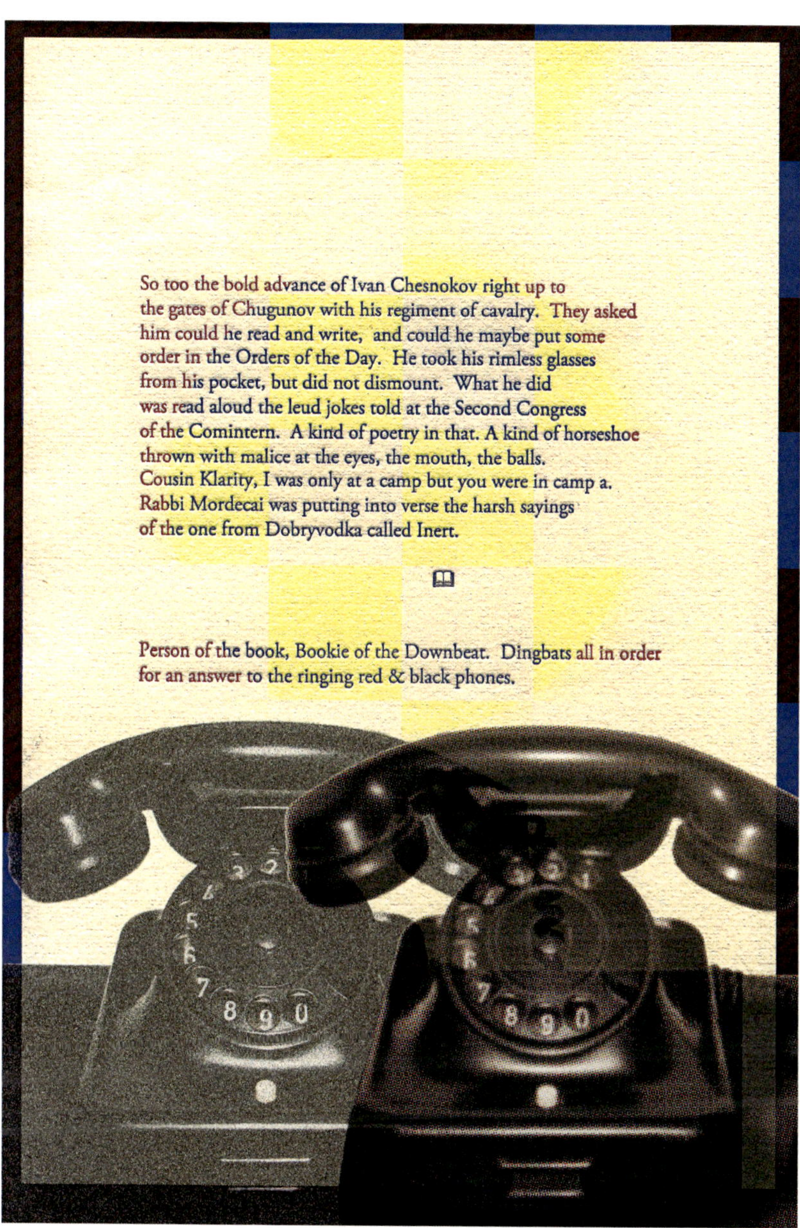

A is for Zukofsky

Like Matthias, Louis Zukofsky drew much from Pound, including the impulses to write from history, to write of beauty caught in or flying from the web of politics, and to write in series. In the twelfth section of his greatest, longest poem, "*A*," he mimics Bach—working mutations, much as Bach did at the end of *The Art of the Fugue*, on the recurring letters B, A, C, and H. Matthias, too, cares for mutation. Consider his mutations of Mandelstam. Consider in particular the fate of the Russian poet's knucklebones.

In "He Who Finds a Horseshoe," children play with found bones—redeeming the lostness of the past, making from the long-dead something ludic, something live:

> A rustle runs through the trees, a verdant ball-game:
> Children play knucklebones with the vertebrae from
>   beasts gone extinct,
> The brittle time of our era comes
>
>   to an end.

In Matthias' poem, the children become officers, the found bones dingbats:

> He stumbled bleeding
> into foreign camp where all the officers played
> dice with nasty dingbats, bits of backbone
>   lacking, they maintained,
> in cowards who'd run off.

A transformation from Mandelstam's world of play to a darkened world of power, from freedom to confinement and cruelty—a variant on the dialectic of those forces readers can find throughout Matthias' work. That dialectic in Matthias?

It's something like his DNA. I don't want to talk of play and power, though—I want to talk about mutation, about the change of DNA.

Mandelstam's knucklebones mutate to dingbats, and mutate yet again into another kind of dingbat—the symbols, derived from typography, one finds in the Symbol menu of an Apple MacBook pro. Matthias scatters them throughout his poem: 💣, we find, or 📖, or ☎ or ✏ or ✂✇ "I think of them as sucking-stones," Matthias says, adding "Demosthenes sucked stones" (he did: an obstacle to oratory, to make him practice well).

💣, in particular, interests: it has a history with Apple Macs. In the old days, it's what you got on your screen when the system crashed, and any work not saved in memory was gone, and gone for good. The notion of lost memory haunts "After Five Words Englished From the Russian," a poem thick with neurobiology, and rising out of the time in Matthias' life when his wife's neurological health had faltered. Matthias invokes "aplasia," when discussing this neurological failure, a term for the failure of an organism to grow, change, or develop. A failure, one might say, of mutation and change. Against cessation, against the system crash, against the evaporation of memory in the presence of a neural 💣, we have mutation—the making of the old things new.

Mandelstam found, in Dante, the "unrivaled master of transmutable and convertible poetic material." He didn't want to preserve what Dante wrote, so much as to draw from it, morph it, keep it live and make it new. Matthias morphs Mandelstam's knucklebones, makes a mutation from the older poet's work. Against the system crash that destroys memory, against aplasia's stasis—something stirring, something live. (One might characterize the matter with the icons of creativity arrayed against the icon of violent crash, as 📖, ☎, ✐ and ☏ vs. 💣).

 Like a child in a Russian forest, Matthias plays with what was dead, to break the brittleness of time.

III

Picks up the black: *Name and patronymic.* You think all this
security is just a game?   Interrogation's terminal.
Means you integrate, and don't fill out that line on race.
Do fill out the item re your mother's maiden name. Tartar, no?
When I first went to Paris with the orderly for mess
we asked for steak tartare. Didn't know the local customs, raw egg
on raw meat. Nearly barfed, but stayed cool, & ate it up.
Did you clean your plate at camp? No you can't phone Mother now.
You'll answer only to the bad cop at mass. I hope for
your sake, Soldier, all of this can be resolved as expeditiously
as possible.
           Hello up there & looking disingenuous
and fat. Here's a joke. Guy goes to a shrink. After a while
the shrink says, Man you're absolutely nuts. Man says Please sir
I'd like a second opinion. Shrink says OK, Man, you're
bloody ugly too. Man says, Mein Herr, but I'm the Revolution
of the Word. Shrink says: Well then speak

III

Picks up the black: *Name and patronymic.* You think all this
security is just a game?   Interrogation's terminal.
Means you integrate, and don't fill out that line on race.
Do fill out the item re your mother's maiden name. Tartar, no?
When I first went to Paris with the orderly for mess
we asked for steak tartare. Didn't know the local customs, raw egg
on raw meat. Nearly barfed, but stayed cool, & ate it up.
Did you clean your plate at camp? No you can't phone Mother now.
You'll answer only to the bad cop at mass. I hope for
your sake, Soldier, all of this can be resolved as expeditiously
as possible.
                    Hello up there & looking disingenuous
and fat. Here's a joke. Guy goes to a shrink. After a while
the shrink says, Man you're absolutely nuts. Man says Please sir
I'd like a second opinion. Shrink says OK, Man, you're
bloody ugly too. Man says, Mein Herr, but I'm the Revolution
of the Word. Shrink says: Well then speak

Horseshoe **to hoarsepshaw**

Name and patronymic. You think all this
security is just a game? Interrogation's terminal

We begin here with trouble or, more specifically, in
trouble. In trouble with power, which turns language into its
instrument. Interrogation is decidedly not a matter of play,
security no mere game. Our hero (a kind of avatar of Mandel-
stam) is looking at detention, deportation, and death in the
camps. The end. But then there's this: "Means you integrate,
and don't fill out that line on race." We've moved from "inter-
rogation" to "integrate," and for no apparent reason having
to do with plot. There's a bit of the ludic involved, Matthias
moving from one word to another based on the resemblance
of sounds—an ancient form of word play and, through such
devices as rhyme, a central one for poetry. Security may well be
no game, but language, for Matthias? Well, it can be. He plays
a little more in the lines that follow:

> Do fill out the item re your mother's maiden name.
>   Tartar, no?
> When I first went to Paris with the orderly for mess
> we asked for steak tartare. Didn't know the local
>   customs, raw egg
> on raw meat. Nearly barfed, but stayed cool, & ate it up.

On the one hand, the Tartar nature of the interrogatee's
mother's maiden name ties us into the Mandelstam story (his
lover, Anna Akhmatova, claimed Tartar ancestry. On the other
hand, it's real function is simply to connect us to food (the
steak tartare) and, via food, bring about a segue from the mat-
ter of Mandelstam to Matthias' own experiences at summer
camp, where he, in his own way, was subject to arbitrary power.
The resemblance of the two words is the occasion to show us a
resemblance of biographical events.

This slipping about, following the leads generated by linguistic resemblances, by sound-echoes, is at the heart of that form of play known as poetry found in "After Five Words Englished from the Russian." Indeed, the poem announces this at its very beginning, when we move from Mandelstam's "horseshoe" to Matthias' "hoarsepshaw."

*

If I were to continue this commentary by glossing the rest of the passage from "After Five Words Englished from the Russian," I would say something about how the psychiatrist represents a figure of power ("Mein Herr"), subjecting our hero to his discipline. I would add something about our hero's attempt to resist this power by claiming to be "the Revolution of the Word," and relate that revolution to playful sound-echoes and word mutations of the sort we've seen: horseshoe/hoarsepshaw, etc. I'd end with some meditation or other about the psychiatrist commanding our hero to speak, thus indicating Matthias' ambivalence about the nature of the verbal revolution: if our hero chooses to use language after this command, he is no longer in revolt, but obeying an order. Of course he could use words in ways so revolutionary they could hardly be considered speech (is "hoarsepshaw" a word, really, and if so, what kind, and how?"). But I don't want to do any of this. I want to do something different.

*

I want to quote Roman Jakobson, from his essay on aphasia (a theme close to the heart of the man who wrote "Five Words Englished from the Russian), "Two Aspects of Language and Two Types of Disturbances." Here's what Jabobson says:

79

Every form of aphasic disturbance consists in some impairment, more or less severe, either of the faculty for selection and substitution or for combination and contexture. The former affliction involves a deterioration of metalinguistic operations, while the latter damages the capacity for maintaining the hierarchy of linguistic units. The relation of similarity is suppressed in the former, the relation of contiguity in the latter type of aphasia.

An impairment of the faculty of combination stops one from making coherent sentences—try diagramming the sentences of certain of our political figures, and you will find ample evidence of such impairment. An impairment of the faculty of selection prevents one from being able to choose the correct word: if one cannot think, for example, of a synonym for a given word, one is suffering (perhaps only momentarily) this form of aphasia. For Jakobson, the ability to make metaphors shows that one is free of aphasia in the faculty of selection: one can speak of a journey, and substitute for it any word that might make for a metaphoric equivalent: *pilgrimage,* or *drift.*

But what if our faculty isn't for near-equivalents of sense, so much as for near-equivalents of sound? Is this aphasia, or its cure? On what journey will this take us? On what pilgrimage or drift? To where?

He who finds a hoarsepshaw knows the way.

                                              He doesn't though,
he can't. He's gagged by then. And look at how
his hands are tied behind him. If he could speak he'd
improvise a panegyric on his old Prof. Then they'd let him off.
For example, Camper Klubnik might begin, speaking as a
prisoner in the nether fields of play: *By God they had me walk
upon the water, bored. That made all of them electric.*
The men in protective cover took *Aplysia* by the tail & shocked
him good, found that serotonin is a modulator and that
neurons form connections where a new protein is required
for growth. Our team, my Champion, seeks out
long-term memory: Your own. Our mistake in Paris was in
not ordering the snails in white wine sauce.
(If you'll just attach those wires to his name and patronymic
we can all go home)
                              Camp A is not ballet in Voronezh,
although it's true they have a company. The dance we'll do
together's called the Nimble Neurons. Simple stimulation with
the horseshoe, hard. The Presbyterian (head) Master
got so angry that he cast dung about him, rang the orthodox bell,

hid the weapon in the tall grass of long-term mnemonics,
left it there to find. Fend for yourself, my boy, who called him friend.

he can't. He's gagged by then. And look at how
his hands are tied behind him. If he could speak he'd
improvise a panegyric on his old Prof. Then they'd let him off.
For example, Camper Klubnik might begin, speaking as a
prisoner in the nether fields of play: *By God they had me walk
upon the water, bored. That made all of them electric.*
The men in protective cover took *Aplysia* by the tail & shocked
him good, found that serotonin is a modulator and that
neurons form connections where a new protein is required
for growth. Our team, my Champion, seeks out
long-term memory: Your own. Our mistake in Paris was in
not ordering the snails in white wine sauce.
(If you'll just attach those wires to his name and patronymic
we can all go home)

        Camp A is not ballet in Voronezh,
although it's true they have a company. The dance we'll do
together's called the Nimble Neurons. Simple stimulation with
the horseshoe, hard. The Presbyterian (head) Master
got so angry that he cast dung about him, rang the orthodox bell,

hid the weapon in the tall grass of long-term mnemonics,
left it there to find. Fend for yourself, my boy, who called him friend.

After five years of silence

> But I'm the Revolution
> Of the Word. Shrink says: Well then speak

>   He doesn't though,
> he can't. He's gagged by then. And look at how
> his hands are tied behind him. If he could speak he'd
> improvise a panegyric on his old Prof. Then they'd let
> him off.

If only one could speak, and praise the right person, one could
go free. If only they hadn't gagged you already for your Revolu-
tion of the Word. If only you hadn't been forced into a silence…

*

In 1930, after five years of silence in which he wrote
nothing, Mandelstam picked up his pen and wrote again:

> On the island of Sevan, which is conspicuous for two
> most dignified architectural monuments that date back
> to the seventh century, as well as for mud huts of flea-
> bitten hermits only recently passed away, thickly over-
> grown with nettles and thistles, but no more frighten-
> ing than the neglected cellars of summer houses. I spent
> a month enjoying the lake water that stood at a height
> of four thousand feet above sea level and training my-
> self to contemplate the two or three dozen tombs…

This was his start of his *Journey to Armenia.* You'd think the
poem would begin with more optimism: the journey, after all,
crosses the Caucasus from Abkhazia to Armenia—meaning
this is the territory where Jason's Argonauts found the Golden
Fleece, which will place Jason on his rightful throne. The

journey also takes Mandelstam to Mount Ararat, where Noah
and the few just survivors of the flood came to rest, and began
life anew. But perhaps it's best that Mandelstam begins with
tombs, ruins, and the mud huts of dead hermits. After five
years of silence he was writing again, but in less than three years
he'd write his Stalin epigram. After that—no mounting of the
rightful throne, no survival to begin life anew. The journey that
began in Abkhazia led him to writing, yes, but writing led him
to a Gulag transit camp, where he disappeared.

*

If only one had been silent, not disparaged the person
who deserved it most, one might have remained free. If by free
one means silenced. If by free one means a flea-bitten hermit in
a mud hut, thickly overgrown with nettles and thistles.

*

Helen Vendler tells us that Mandelstam,

> …after five years during which he was unable to
> compose, discovered for himself that writing about
> anything at all—provided one writes as a free man
> uncoerced by political prudence—is itself a rebuke to
> the totalitarian attempt to govern the writer's tongue,
> to direct writing toward certain approved subjects.

And so the huts of Armenian hermits rebuke Stalin, and are
a form of freedom greater than what would have resulted for
Matthias' Mandelstam-ish hero, had he been ungagged long
enough to praise his prof. It is pretty to think so. It is the
hermit's fondest dream: his mud hut an ark; his flea-bitten flesh
itself a golden fleece.

85

IV

Picks up the red: *Koba Steel here. . . .* (No, not a CEO.)
So stop and think. You're at a high point in telephonic history.
He asks you now about your friend. Wants to know
is he the Big One. For a moment you are overcome by envy.
Iosif the Georgian – Koba, Mr. Steel – thinks your
friend and rival maybe is the Big One. He's waiting for your
answer on the phone. *Horseshoe, you know I don't . . .*

So think again. You're having dinner with some friends
And Джугашвили (-shvili is the suffix meaning *child*)
telephones and asks you is your rival really great.
It isn't Harry Truman on the line, not General Eisenhower,
not even J. Edger Hoover. It's the Ossetian, *the herd of sheep.*
Yet another name is сталь, suffix -ин You've heard of sheep,
but not from Georgia. (Georgia doesn't border Florida.)
He takes an avid interest in the welfare of the motherland's bards.
Three times blessed is one who puts a name in song.
Boris Leonidovich, for example.

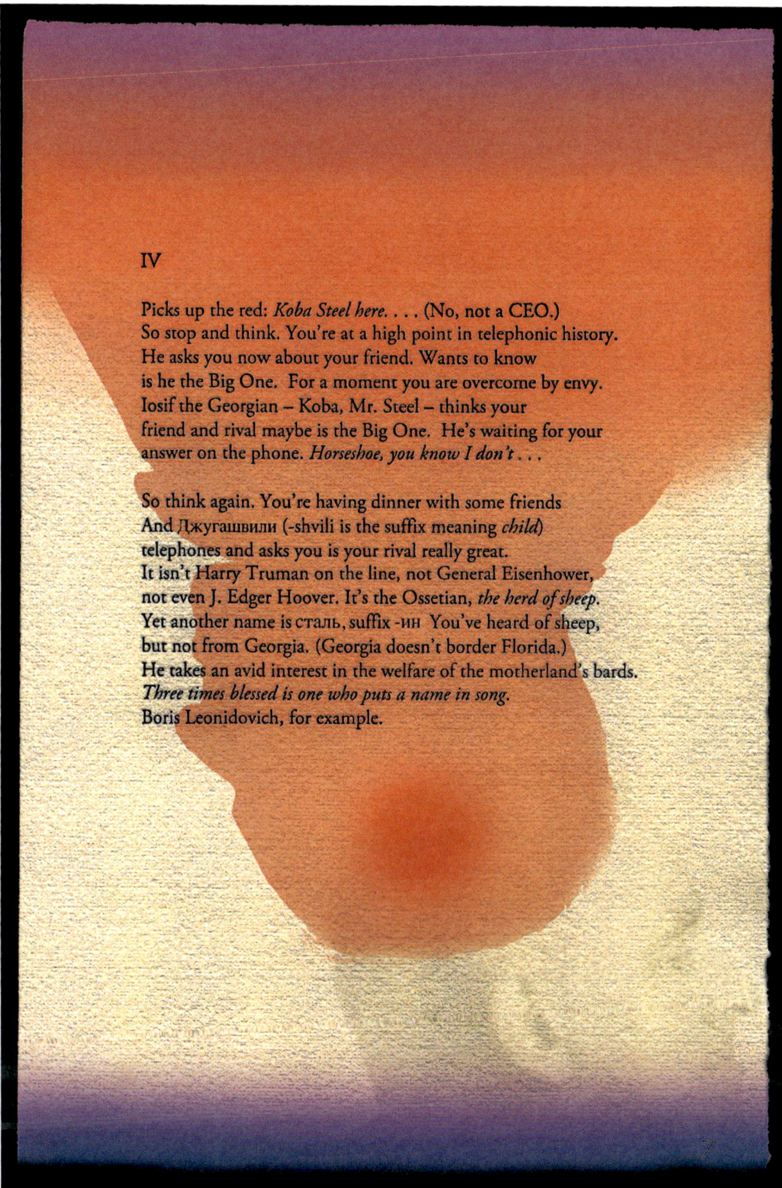

IV

Picks up the red: *Koba Steel here. . . .* (No, not a CEO.)
So stop and think. You're at a high point in telephonic history.
He asks you now about your friend. Wants to know
is he the Big One. For a moment you are overcome by envy.
Iosif the Georgian – Koba, Mr. Steel – thinks your
friend and rival maybe is the Big One. He's waiting for your
answer on the phone. *Horseshoe, you know I don't . . .*

So think again. You're having dinner with some friends
And Джугашвили (-shvili is the suffix meaning *child*)
telephones and asks you is your rival really great.
It isn't Harry Truman on the line, not General Eisenhower,
not even J. Edger Hoover. It's the Ossetian, *the herd of sheep.*
Yet another name is сталь, suffix -ин You've heard of sheep,
but not from Georgia. (Georgia doesn't border Florida.)
He takes an avid interest in the welfare of the motherland's bards.
Three times blessed is one who puts a name in song.
Boris Leonidovich, for example.

Words for **Stalin**

Iosif Besarionis dze Jughashvili, born December 18th, 1878; died March 5, 1973 (not soon enough).

*

-shvili is the suffix meaning "child," or "son"—as in Johnson, Anderson. But "Jugha" or "Dzugha"? Some say it means "steel" (which it doesn't). Some, who like neither Stalin nor the Jews, have said that it means "Jew." In truth, there is no such word as "Jugha" in Georgian. But some say it isn't a Georgian word, but from an Ossetian dialect: the word for "sheep herd" or the word for "trash." I like that last one. Go with that.

*

His friends called him "Soselo" or "Soso," diminutive for "Iosef." He had friends. Then he had power.

*

He was also called "Vozhd," for "leader," a loan word to modern Russian from the old Orthodox Church Slavonic, and so redolent of a bishop's sanctity, or of a Moses to lead us to a promised land.

*

He liked nicknames, especially "The Red Tsar," taken for reasons clear enough. He'd add the royals to the ecclesiastics in his roll-call for himself, though he'd helped to kill both sorts, and more.

88

*

"Dear Father," many called him. As in a prayer for mercy, as in a prayer of fear.

*

He chose "Stalin" because it meant "steel." That much was true.

*

It was the Americans who called him "Uncle Joe," but Harry Truman called him "little squirt." And that was true as well.

*

But "Koba" was the first, the nickname that he loved. His father was a drunk who beat his wife and son, and when little Soso took to running with a gang of racketeers, he dreamed of fighting back. He read *The Patricide*, a Georgian novel, and stole its hero's name. So Soso was now Koba. Some say he killed papa.

*

Matthias gives us "Koba," "Steel," "the Big One," "Iosif," a Cyrillic "Jughashvili." He gives us "herd of sheep." He also quotes from Mandelstam, "*Three times blessed is one who puts a name in song.*" These names? One thinks he means the other one, "Boris Leonidovich." That's someone worth a blessing: Pasternak.

But who gives a blessing for one like Pasternak, one who, like Mandelstam, "writes as a free man uncoerced by political prudence"? Who sees such a man as "a rebuke to the totalitarian attempt to govern the writer's tongue, to direct writing toward certain approved subjects"? Who sees him and will bless his name?

A hermit does, in his mud hut ark, his flea-bitten flesh itself a golden fleece. Matthias does. Me too.

He says, *I think you liked the summer camp we sent you to.*
We gave you a dacha all your own; not a day, not an hour
did you spend like some Denisovich. You know. You're grateful,
But you've got these dinner guests. *Koba, we will have*
To keep it short. You're so frightened now you're shitting in
Your pants. *Can we take this up another time?*
You feel gagged, and look at how your hands are tied
behind you so you have to cradle the contrivance
with your chin. *Boris Leonidovich, have a pleasant meal.*

An old camp counselor, a bully Boy Scout grown into
a what? A what?
          . . . writing for him on Yagoda-Checkist
checker board, black squares and red, king makers, triple jumps,
a bowl of raspberries lodged in each man's lap, a rasp
in both voices, a rattle then: *Were I to take my pencil up for*
the supremist praise, I would speak of him who shifts the
axis of the world and call him by his dobrydawnsong name,
Dzhugashvili

Koba was a *nom de guerre*, and he darkened eighteen others.
Dzhugashvili only an aubade.

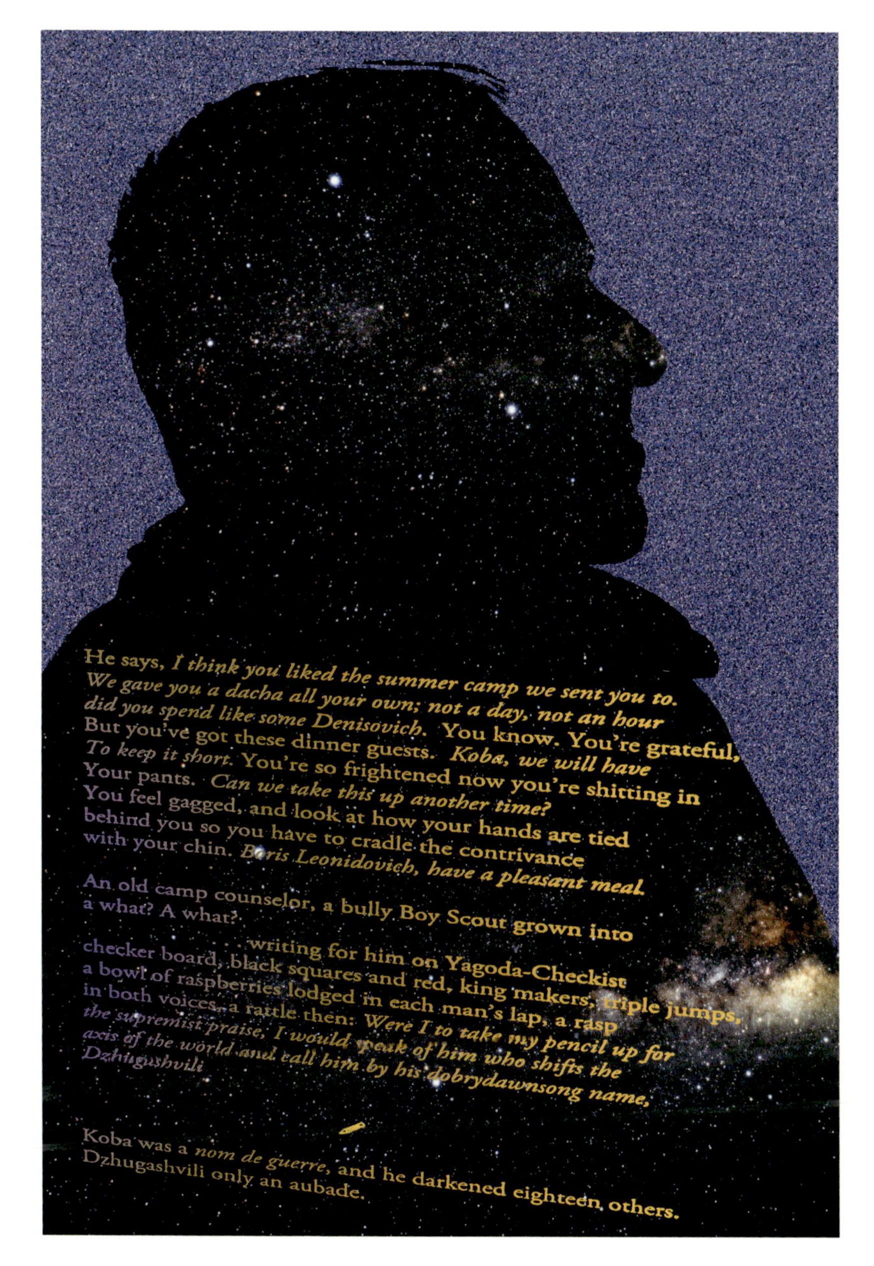

He says, *I think you liked the summer camp we sent you to.*
We gave you a dacha all your own; not a day, not an hour
did you spend like some Denisovich. You know. You're grateful,
But you've got these dinner guests. *Koba, we will have*
To keep it short. You're so frightened now you're shitting in
Your pants. *Can we take this up another time?*
You feel gagged, and look at how your hands are tied
behind you so you have to cradle the contrivance
with your chin. *Boris Leonidovich, have a pleasant meal.*

An old camp counselor, a bully Boy Scout grown into
a what? A what?

            writing for him on Yagoda-Checkist
checker board, black squares and red, king makers, triple jumps,
a bowl of raspberries lodged in each man's lap, a rasp
in both voices, a rattle then: *Were I to take my pencil up for*
the supremist praise, I would speak of him who shifts the
axis of the world and call him by his dobrydawnsong name,
Dzhugashvili

Koba was a *nom de guerre,* and he darkened eighteen others.
Dzhugashvili only an aubade.

Englished, or: the fate of John Matthias

John Matthias is an Englished American.

Matthias, born in that dullest of American cities, Columbus, sought escape in a thousand ways: into absorptive play, into French existentialism, to Turkey on a youthful journey, to California for grad school. But where he truly found escape was England. The glamor of the place for him was, initially, literary—as it has been for many literary Americans before and since. He wanted to write about Auden and Spender, wanted to know a thing or two about Bloomsbury. He wanted, I think, to step in from outside—and literature in America is always on the outside edge of things. But the glamor of England soon became less abstract: indeed, it was made flesh. Matthias met Diana Adams, soon to be his wife, and through her came another kind of English glamor: parties with her relative, a lord, and summers in a long, thatched house in Suffolk, where he'd write of ley lines, flint knappers, the soil itself. It was his otherworld, this England, away from the barbaric America where he and his students were gassed by the rioting Chicago police, where he felt the powers closing in on his friends.

But Matthias' England was always also something else. It was a way to bounce his American experience off something different, to squint and see it from another angle. And it's all angles, with Matthias. A wonderfully perceptive critic once wrote:

> From his earliest poems to his most recent, we find Matthias changing his perspective on experiences—often difficult or painful ones—by placing them in the context of distant geographies, remote pasts, or foreign lives. Even the erotic poetry of Matthias' youth works this way. Consider "What They Say," a short poem written when Matthias was twenty and published for the first time

in volume one of the *Collected Shorter Poems*. Grouped with other erotic poems like "Female Nude, Young" and "Swimming at Midnight," it describes the Viennese painter Egon Schiele in his studio, posing his models and friends as "onanistic nudes," then climbing a ladder to a loft to get the odd angle he desired. "And it's the perspective that distorts," writes Matthias, "The ladder and the beds/were Egon Schiele's." while "The postures and/the gestures/were all theirs." It's a simple poem, and very much juvenilia, but in a way it contains the poetic career that will follow for another half century and more. It's not just that Matthias' erotic imagination, here, runs toward the visions of long-dead artists in faraway Europe rather than the proximate body of a lover: it's that the important thing, the thing that makes Schiele more than a pornographer, is his distancing himself from his material, his climbing of a ladder to gain exactly the right point of distance and perspective.

All quite true. But what of the present context—what of the camps? *"I think you liked the summer camp we sent you to./We gave you a dacha all your own; not a day, not an hour/did you spend like some Denisovich."* Those are words from an imagined (and anachronistic, given the reference to Solzhenitsyn's *A Day in the Life of Ivan Denisovich*) version of Mandelstam's life, his journey to the Gulag. But the other camp, the one with "An old camp counselor, a bully Boy Scout grown into/a what? A what?" is Matthias' own camp experience as a child under the thumb of a sadistic camp administrator. To get an angle on all that, Matthias climbs a ladder named "Mandelstam."

This time out, Matthias isn't Englished, but Russianed. But whether Egon Schiele's ladder is England or Russia, it begins where all the ladders start, the foul rag and bone shop of the heart.

V

The telephone, the book, the pencil, and the bomb.
The horseshoe, the letter Ж, Aplysia, a prod. Full stop, Aplasia
No codes where none intended.
No modes where all roads lead to home. No Rome.
Beneath her stone,
                    Arachne spins an Achmeist revival.
Rest with mother, bested brother,
shining on a harvest moon. Frost at midnight, steel
reflecting starlight: Stella, Stalin, Blog-
meister Ulyanov. *He Who Finds a Horseshoe*
fires a synapse, begs a question, bags his quarry in due time
but fears it was a 💣   Nihilism was your nickelodeon, Clarity
embracing nil, your dingbat more than that
but only half the whole.
                    The other half in plus fours
Told it as a crime, a time when the brakeman was annoyed
at Nickerbocker, who was there for re-hab
in the -ilitation for an injury sustained to his cerebral cortex
from the wreck of nations on the railroad track that
used to be an outback songline, wrack of notions that were
once all viable ideals, and so he hit him HARD
with what was handy: *horseshoe*. He could have put him
In a
      📖

        or gouged out his eye with a
                              ✏️

V

The telephone, the book, the pencil, and the bomb.
The horseshoe, the letter Ж, Aplysia, a prod. Full stop, Aplasia
No codes where none intended.
No modes where all roads lead to home. No Rome.
Beneath her stone,
                    Arachne spins an Achmeist revival.
Rest with mother, bested brother,
shining on a harvest moon. Frost at midnight, steel
reflecting starlight: Stella, Stalin, Blog-
meister Ulyanov. *He Who Finds a Horseshoe*
fires a synapse, begs a question, bags his quarry in due time
but fears it was a 🐎.   Nihilism was your nickelodeon, Clarity
embracing nil, your dingbat more than that
but only half the whole.
                        The other half in plus fours
Told it as a crime, a time when the brakeman was annoyed
at Nickerbocker, who was there for re-hab
in the -ilitation for an injury sustained to his cerebral cortex
from the wreck of nations on the railroad track that
used to be an outback songline, wrack of notions that were
once all viable ideals, and so he hit him HARD
with what was handy: *horseshoe*. He could have put him
In a 📖

              or gouged out his eye with a

97

From Mandelstam to Matthias

From a leather merchant's house in Warsaw (the Pale of
Settlement) to St. Petersburg. And how?
From a special dispensation
(from the Tsar).
From there, the Tenishevsky School,
from which came Nabokov.
From there, to Paris (la Sorbonne).
From there to Heidelberg.
From Judaism to Methodism.
From which conversion: admittance, the University in St. Petersburg.
From populist to symbolist.
From schemes with Gumilyov and Gorodetsky, a circle and a
plan: *The Morning of Acmeism.*
From his pen, *The Stone.*
From lust, his Anna (Akhmativa).
From her to a princess (Salomea).
From there to love, to Nadezhda Yakovlevna, to marry her in old Kiev.
From her bed to Olga's,
From hers on to Maria's.
From hers to more, and many more.
From outrage, an epigram. "The Kremlin Mountaineer."
From then, just trouble, and to jail and in Cherdyn.
From a suicide attempt to further exile.
From exile *Poems of an Unknown Soldier,* and an invitation to a farm.

From there, abduction, to a camp (Vtoraya Rechka),

From which he sent a letter to his wife.

From there (at 47) disappeared.

From there, immortal as a poet martyr, martyred Jew.

From there to many places, even here.

*

John Matthias comes from Republican Ohio, and got out.

All the way to California. All the way to England.

And all the way back, almost, almost.

He isn't Mandelstam. He wanted me to tell you that knows.

These are conventions that you see in
Children's books. Child Aplasia failed all exams.
Aplysia *could* respond. But where exactly in these snail brains
did one locate the long-term memory, let alone the Ego
and the Id? Could they, anyway, be trained by pain, subjective
and unconscious? (No codes where none intended.
No allusions that have not offended. No mimesis. No thesis.)
If you cross synoptic cleft, target ion channel and inject
The catalytic element, you're under way. Dingbat is an object
used as missile in the absence of a horseshoe.
Or a gizmogadget with an utterly forsaken ancient name.
A typographical ornament . A silly jerk. A slug releasing ink.

What I'm saying isn't said by me.
This is your whingding moment: dug out of the ground like
gold.

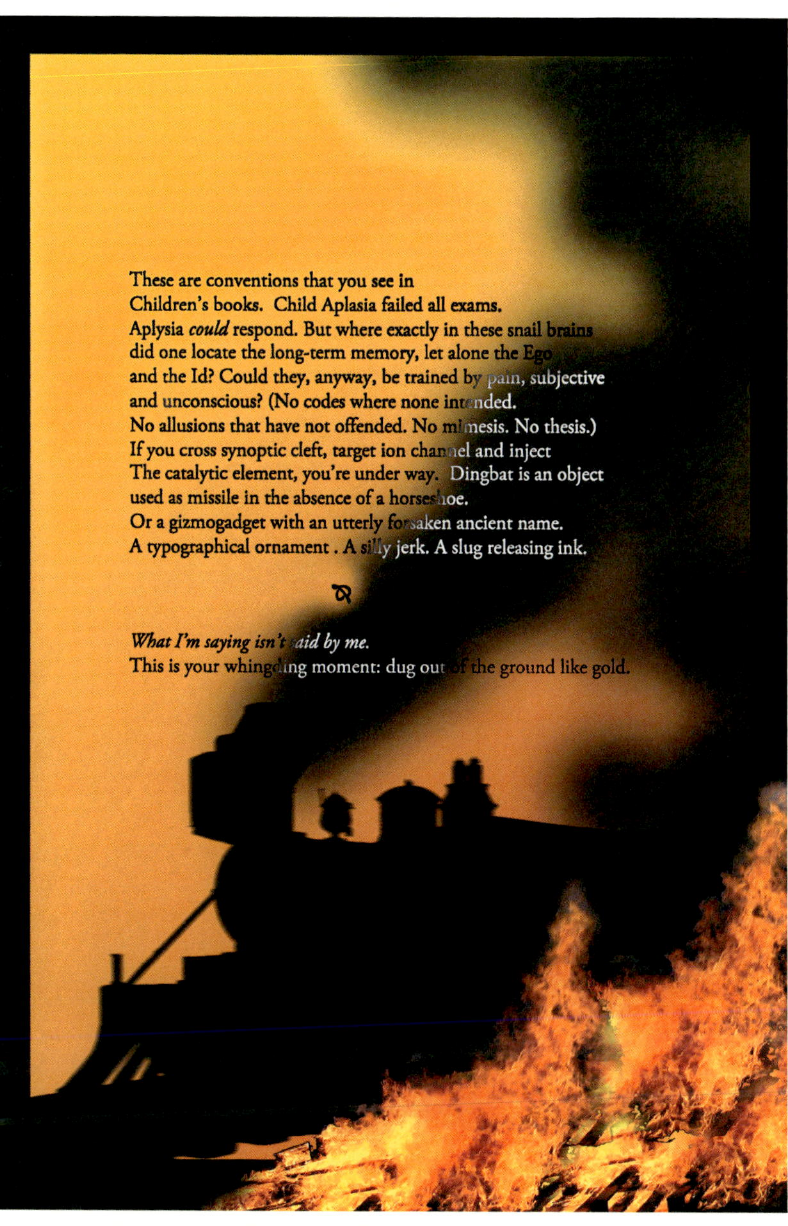

These are conventions that you see in
Children's books. Child Aplasia failed all exams.
Aplysia *could* respond. But where exactly in these snail brains
did one locate the long-term memory, let alone the Ego
and the Id? Could they, anyway, be trained by pain, subjective
and unconscious? (No codes where none intended.
No allusions that have not offended. No mimesis. No thesis.)
If you cross synoptic cleft, target ion channel and inject
The catalytic element, you're under way. Dingbat is an object
used as missile in the absence of a horseshoe.
Or a gizmogadget with an utterly forsaken ancient name.
A typographical ornament . A silly jerk. A slug releasing ink.

What I'm saying isn't said by me.
This is your whingding moment: dug out of the ground like gold.

The Russian

(Пиндарический отрывок)

Глядим на лес и говорим:
- Вот лес корабельный, мачтовый,
Розовые сосны,
До самой верхушки свободные от мохнатой ноши,
Им бы поскрипывать в бурю,
Одинокими пиниями,
В разъяренном безлесном воздухе;
Под соленою пятою ветра устоит отвес,
           пригнанный к пляшущей палубе,
И мореплаватель,
В необузданной жажде пространства,
Влача через влажные рытвины хрупкий
              прибор геометра,
Сличит с притяженьем земного лона
Шероховатую поверхность морей.

А вдыхая запах
Смолистых слез, проступивших сквозь
             обшивку корабля,
Любуясь на доски
Заклепанные, слаженные в переборки
Не вифлеемским мирным плотником,
           а другим -
Отцом путешествий, другом морехода,-
Говорим:
    - И они стояли на земле,
Неудобной, как хребет осла,
Забывая верхушками о корнях
На знаменитом горном кряже,
И шумели под пресным ливнем,
Безуспешно предлагая небу выменять

                        на щепотку соли
Свой благородный груз.

С чего начать?
Всё трещит и качается.
Воздух дрожит от сравнений.
Ни одно слово не лучше другого,
Земля гудит метафорой,
И легкие двуколки,
В броской упряжи густых от натуги птичьих
                                стай,
Разрываются на части,
Соперничая с храпящими любимцами
                        ристалищ.

Трижды блажен, кто введет в песнь имя;
Украшенная названьем песнь

Дольше живет среди других -
Она отмечена среди подруг повязкой на лбу,
Исцеляющий от беспамятства, слишком
                        сильного
одуряющего запаха -
Будь то близость мужчины,
Или запах шерсти сильного зверя,
Или просто дух чебра, растертого между
                        ладоней.

Воздух бывает темным, как вода, и всё живое
в нем плавает, как рыба,
Плавниками расталкивая сферу,
Плотную, упругую, чуть нагретую,-
Хрусталь, в котором движутся колеса
                и шарахаются лошади,

Влажный чернозем Нееры, каждую ночь
                               распаханный заново
Вилами, трезубцами, мотыгами, плугами.
Воздух замешен так же густо, как земля,-
Из него нельзя выйти, в него трудно войти.

Шорох пробегает по деревьям зеленой
                               лаптой:
Дети играют в бабки позвонками умерших
                               животных.
Хрупкое исчисление нашей эры подходит
                               к концу.
Спасибо за то, что было:
Я сам ошибся, я сбился, запутался в счете.
Эра звенела, как шар золотой,
Полая, литая, никем не поддерживаемая,
На всякое прикосновение отвечала
                               "да" и "нет".
Так ребенок отвечает:
"Я дам тебе яблоко" или "Я не дам тебе
                               яблока".
И лицо его точный слепок с голоса, который
                               произносит эти слова.

Звук еще звенит, хотя причина звука исчезла.
Конь лежит в пыли и храпит в мыле,
Но крутой поворот его шеи
Еще сохраняет воспоминание о беге
                               с разбросанными ногами,-
Когда их было не четыре,
А по числу камней дороги,
Обновляемых в четыре смены,
По числу отталкивании от земли пышущего
                               жаром иноходца.

Так
Нашедший подкову
Сдувает с нее пыль
И растирает ее шерстью, пока она
                          не заблестит,
Тогда
Он вешает ее на пороге,
Чтобы она отдохнула,
И больше уж ей не придется высекать
                          искры из кремня.
Человеческие губы, которым больше нечего
                              сказать,
Сохраняют форму последнего сказанного
                              слова,
И в руке остается ощущенье тяжести,
Хотя кувшин
          наполовину расплескался,
                    пока его несли
                          домой.

То, что я сейчас говорю, говорю не я,
А вырыто из земли, подобно зернам
                    окаменелой пшеницы.
Одни
      на монетах изображают льва,
Другие -
      голову.
Разнообразные медные, золотые и бронзовые
                              лепешки
С одинаковой почестью лежат в земле;
Век, пробуя их перегрызть, оттиснул на них
                              свои зубы.
Время срезает меня, как монету,
И мне уж не хватает меня самого.

Epilogue: The Age

Fangled bitch, my Age, who will ever gaze
into your wolfish whiskered face?
Whose blood the glue to stick your backbones
back together after two millennia?
Maker's blood splashes from the old passport
into mug of whore Age's desperate case.
On prison sills of grim future's coin, spends
a hanging man his comfort's lot.

*

Cannot stop the blood maker's flood
from gushing into everything that lives and dies,
ill-ebbed of floodtides, tossing fire-fish
on the sea-bone sodden sand,
while above it all the netted songbirds bride-
sing the sorrow as it pours and pours,
fangled bitch, my Age,
upon your wounded living dying hide.

*

Wolf whiskers bristle at the blood maker's
Word, but torn away by singing flute that
founds bondage on the Age itself, binding
all the musics into grief and coin, backbones
broken into mortal days, measure into fear
and prosody, rattling vertebrae you'd hear
from steeltown or city, country house
or mousehole – here, there – or anywhere.

*

Assailed is a word. And so is *asylum*.
Thrice blessed is he who puts a name in his poem:
Osip, Anna, John. Twenty sticks drop down from
Giants playing six dimensional YiJing.
But also blessed is he who writes *refrain, refrain.*
Sing me, sergeant, to the unscheduled train.
I think I'd tell you almost anything,
shuffling barefoot feet in octave, mud, and rain.

J.M., after O.M.

A few notes on the project

1.

The final shape of this book came together slowly over the last several years. I do not remember the exact year when I wrote "The HIJ," but it was finished in time for a reading of the full cycle at Clare Hall, Cambridge, in 2010 and for inclusion as the last poem in my *Collected Shorter Poems*, Vol. 2, in 2011. "After Five Words Englished from the Russian" followed more or less immediately, and was published in the inaugural issue of the *Huffington Post Literary Supplement* and as the final poem in my *Collected Longer Poems*, 2012 in both instances. In 2014 Jean Dibble expressed interest in making poster poems from the texts of "The HIJ"; these were exhibited in a presentation, along with many collaborations from the past with Douglas Kinsey, in the Notre Dame Library Department of Special Collections. In 2016 Jean Dibble's poster poems appeared on the *X-Peri* web site. When she went on to make poster poems from "After Five Words Englished from the Russian," they too were published on *X-Peri* later in the same year.

2.

When the "After Five Words" posters were completed, it appeared that we might have a book. I wanted, however, to add one more element to the mix of texts and art works, and asked Robert Archambeau if he would be interested in writing a series of "free commentaries" on the full run of texts and posters. I suggested that he should write anything he felt like, from analysis through free-association to fiction or automatic writing. The book, to be called *Revolutions: A Collaboration*, would revolve but probably not resolve. That would be okay. Also, it would be understood that all three collaborators were on an equal footing in the book. Posters and "free commentaries" should not be subordinated to the original texts. Indeed, many of Archambeau's "commentaries" are prose poems in their on right and Jean Dibble's posters, framed at full size, can be free-standing art works.

3.

How then should one read the book? I would guess that anyone coming to these works for the first time would very naturally thumb through the posters. Then what? My own preference would be for the reader to return to page one and read the texts *en face*, look again at the adjacent poster poem, and read the commentary, continuing in that way until the book is finished. But I can also imagine a reader who might prefer to read all of the texts straight through, followed then by all of the commentaries. One understands, of course, that readers of poetry books are likely to jump around as it suits them, and that's fine too. All three of us are delighted to have any readers at all, and the reader should feel as "free" as the poet, the artist, or the author of commentaries.

4.

With regard to the "After Five Words" sequence – I do not read Russian. More than that, while working with Osip Mandelstam's great poem "He Who Finds a Horseshoe," I am aware of a trespass. Russian poets and readers are especially protective of Mandelstam when it comes to outsiders like myself. It will also seem to be an outrage, I fear, where my sequence sometimes juxtaposes Mandelstam's experience as a martyr of Stalinism and an American poet's memories of a sadistic camp counselor when he was a child. In the alchemy of composition, this overlap of experiences occurred. W.H. Auden once wrote that his "best reason for opposing fascism" was that at his school he "lived in a fascist state." One summer, terrorized by an ex-professional wrestler working for the YMCA, I lived in the GULAG. Jean Dibble's imagery derives mostly from a photograph of Osip Mandelstam, but the poem is not "about" Mandelstam in the way, for example that Gertrude Schnackenberg's "A Moment in Utopia" is in her book *A Gilded Lapse of Time*. But the poem, wildly associational in many ways, is certainly haunted by Mandelstam's life and work throughout and, in its awkward way, is elegiac.

5.

"There are four of us," wrote Anna Akhmatova in a late poem. They were Mandelstam, Pasternak, Tsvetaeva, and Akhmatova herself. Although, as I have said, I do not read Russian, my wife does. When we first met, Russian poetry had a good deal to do with what we understood about each other. And Russian culture generally. Diana sang for a while in the choir of the London Russian Orthodox Church where she knew many Russian émigrés and admired Bishop Anthony Bloom, a charismatic figure who led many during the 1960s and 1970s to attend his church and even to convert. Diana did not quite convert. One reason may have been that she also attended the cultural events at the Russian Embassy in London, and took me with her. There we drank vodka with "cultural attachés" who were doubtless KGB agents and watched Stalinist musicals. Back in Islington, however, when we began living together, she read me many Russian poems. The Orthodox Church and the Embassy lost their charm, but the poetry stuck, especially the poetry of this remarkable and tragic generation, "the four" of them. Whenever I am reading a translation and want to hear what the original sounds like, all I have to do is ask.

6.

Finally, neurology. I have been a lay student of neurology for thirty years. I do not think philosophy, psychology, or even literature can be understood without it. Because my wife now has Parkinson's disease, I have become obsessive with regard to my studies. What once was interesting is now a requirement of daily living. The presence of "Aplesia" in these texts may seem confusing. The curious reader might Google *Aplysia californica* and see what pops up. The ambitious reader might go on to read Eric R. Kandel's *In Search of Memory: The Emergence of a New Science of Mind* where the author explains the biological basis for memory, and the distinction between short term and long-term memory, while exploring his own life in a remarkable autobiography. We owe a lot to the humble *Aplysia* and the patient experiments of the great neuro-biologist.

J.M.

About the Collaborators

JOHN MATTHIAS has published some thirty books of poetry, translation, criticism, and scholarship. For many years he taught at the University of Notre Dame, where he is still Editor at Large of *Notre Dame Review*. Shearsman Books publishes his three volumes of *Collected Poems*, as well as the uncollected long poem, *Trigons*, his most recent volume of poetry, *Complayntes for Doctor Neuro*, two books of memoirs and literary essays, and the novel, *Different Kinds of Music*.

JEAN DIBBLE is a printmaker and painter who has exhibited extensively, both internationally and nationally since 1978. Recent years have been spent integrating text and image, as well as delving into portraiture. One of the founding members of the Mid America Print Council, a group dedicated to fostering the best in printmaking via conferences, exhibitions, research, and a journal, she has been active in the organization for most of its existence. She teaches all manner of printmaking at the University of Notre Dame.

ROBERT ARCHAMBEAU is a poet and literary critic whose books include the collections *Home and Variations* and *The Kafka Sutra* and the critical studies *Laureates and Heretics, The Poet Resigns: Poetry in a Difficult World* and *Inventions of a Barbarous Age: Poetry from Conceptualism to Rhyme*. He studied with John Matthias at the University of Notre Dame in the 1990s, and taught there and at Lund University in Sweden. He now teaches at Lake Forest College.